Effective Marketing

for the Smaller Business

Effective Marketing

for the Smaller Business

A PRACTICAL GUIDE
By GEOFFREY LACE

SCOPE BOOKS LIMITED

First published May 1982

Scope Books Limited
3 Sandford House, Kingsclere,
Newbury, Berkshire RG15 8PA

British Library Cataloguing in Publication Data

Lace, Geoffrey
   Effective marketing for the smaller business
   1. Marketing
   I. Title
   658.8   HF5415

ISBN 0 906619 13 0

Cover design by Janet Lobban
Typeset by Signland Limited, Farnham, Surrey
Printed and bound in Great Britain by
Billing and Sons Limited
London, Oxford, Worcester

Contents

About the Author

Geoffrey Lace is the Managing Editor of *Marketing* magazine and has been an active member of the Institute of Marketing since 1969, currently sitting on its External Affairs Committee. He has written for many magazines and newspapers on business and related subjects.

After serving in the Royal Air Force he worked in marketing management with smaller companies, including one of his own, for a number of years before his appointment as Chief Executive of the Small Business Bureau, a post he left in early 1980 after four years.

He qualified professionally as a lecturer in marketing and business studies with the University of Manchester and more recently advised small firms on marketing as a consultant to the London Enterprise Agency.

A passionate believer in free enterprise his long-standing interest in smaller businesses has reinforced his firm belief in the vital position they occupy in Britain's economic life, and why the role of effective marketing is so crucial.

Preface

Apart from the expertise required to create a product or service, management of a smaller business in practical terms is based on two disciplines: finance and marketing. There is plenty of help available on financial matters; accountants and bank managers are easily accessible to provide the small business owner and manager with day to day support and practical advice. Not so with marketing. This book sets out to provide business practitioners with a practical guide as to how to introduce effective marketing to their enterprises.

Small business owners and managers have a wide and disparate perception of marketing. Their views range from disinterest − 'I think it has something to do with sales' − to a feeling that marketing is a highly sophisticated skill they intend to implement when they have made their first million and can afford to employ the services of a Harvard graduate! This book is designed to dispel the myths; to show that effective marketing is not only possible, but essential to the wellbeing of *every* business; it will help any firm however large or small and whatever its business.

Most books on marketing devote a great deal of space to defining principles and espousing theory, but not much on the day to day practicalities. It is true that marketing has almost as many definitions as exponents but it is broadly agreed that it is an approach to business management putting the customer before all else. It is a way of thinking but it also involves the application of a multitude of techniques aimed at ensuring the profitable operation of a business in its market.

This book therefore, takes a step by step approach to the functions of marketing, examining each in turn and showing how they are best applied. The facts are presented throughout with the aid of graphs, charts, tables, illustrations and facsimile forms linked in a way that makes the book easy to read. At the end of each chapter there is a simple *Checklist* to be used in conjunction with the information supplied, aimed at encouraging a higher standard of management practice. The book should be *used* as much as read.

But *effective marketing* neither begins nor ends with the successful application of techniques. It also requires thought, research and planning. The book therefore shows what, where and how to research, how to apply this information and ends with a detailed analysis of the *marketing plan*, how to produce it and how to present it. Every businessman knows how vital the marketing plan is, not only as an aid to good management but as a necessary element of the business proposition.

PART I
Introduction

MARKETING
IS FOR ALL
BUSINESSES

1
Approaching Business the Marketing Way

Marketing is concerned with the *profitable* movement of goods and services from the producer right through to the final consumer; but it goes a lot further.

Marketing is a concept — a way of approaching a business and maximising profits; making sure that the business understands its customers and is producing the *right* product or service, selling it to the *right* market at the *right* price. Sadly there are many examples of businesses in Britain selling an inadequate product, at the wrong price to an incomplete market. We need look no further than our ex-motorcycle industry for ample evidence.

Unlike the big firm, marketing for a smaller business is not simply a case of making senior management aware and for them to pass on the day to day operation to middle management. In most small firms there are just not enough resources to employ a Marketing Director and teams of advertising, sales, research and product specialists. Frequently there is only one person responsible for all the functions of marketing, and usually that is only part of the job — he or she will also be running accounts and production, and doing the hiring and firing.

Marketing management can be conveniently divided into a number of functions and it is useful for the small business owner to examine these functions as they apply to his business. Whilst a co-ordinated effort is essential, this functional approach will highlight all possible problems and ensure that the firm's planning and control is most effective. Each function must be carefully analysed and then brought together in a calculated and planned approach to managing the business.

Better marketing will increase profits — not necessarily by increased sales (although it often happens), but by helping the firm to operate more efficiently. For example, a product range might be too large or the discounts too generous, and many firms waste considerable resources on ineffective advertising when a good public relations programme would do better for a fraction of the cost (and, surprisingly, vice versa).

There are no panaceas; not even the most marketing-conscious business is safe from the penalties of inadequate finance or the rigours of deep recession. Marketing is a business philosophy and if the owners, directors and staff use it they are giving themselves the best possible chance of success.

SNODSVILLE — AN OBJECT LESSON

NOTE: The companies, directors and employees in the following story are purely fictional. Unfortunately, SEDATE Ltd and those involved with it bear an all too familiar resemblance to real life.

It just so happens that in Snodsville there are two smallish companies designing, assembling and marketing very similar electronic products. Snodsville is situated in the heart of the vale of the river Snod; it is a bustling town, full of industry, most of it based on new technology.

There is a question on the lips of every business journalist: Is this Britain's answer to Silicon Valley?

Nearby is the University of Snod which prides itself on

having the most advanced Department of Electronics in the world. Many of the country's leading electronic engineers have graduated from Snod and the academic standard of those gaining doctorates is considered second to none, they are all snapped up by large companies at home and abroad.

Past students are encouraged to maintain their links with Snod and each year all are invited to the University for a seminar, and a little light entertainment! It was at one such seminar, 2½ years ago, that a group of ex-students currently working with multi-national companies met to discuss the problems of starting a business.

The session in which they were involved was based on a computer management game and two of them were so fascinated by the project that — quite independently of each other — they decided to go into business for themselves. They both knew that Snodsville Borough Council offered excellent incentives to new businesses starting up on its industrial estate, and both characters felt it would be a good idea to be close to their old university and all its resources.

The two businesses were conceived:

Whizzo Electronics Limited

Founder and Managing Director, Dr William Smart

Smart had been working in the Product Development section of a large computer company. Placed in the middle of a marketing environment he became very much aware of the important role that marketing had played in the undoubted success of his employer. The company even had the foresight to send Smart on a marketing course which although not fully comprehensive had at least taught him the basic principles.

Snodsville Electronic Development And Telecommunications Equipment Limited (SEDATE Ltd)

Founder and Managing Director, Dr Peter Inward

Inward was the best student ever to pass through the University of Snod. He joined a large electronics conglomerate in the design and engineering section where he learnt even more about the design of electronic equipment. He was surrounded by other engineers whom he impressed with his superlative skills, but other than to go home, he did not leave his drawing board and work bench for three years.

Fortunately for both Smart and Inward the University of Snod was very hot on market research. The Professor of Electronics felt that if the University was to play its proper role in technical development it should at least be developing the right thing!

The University had recently received the report of a major survey into telecommunications. It looked mainly at the demand for more sophisticated telephone equipment and assessed the potential market for different types of handsets.

The University made the results of the survey available to Inward and Smart, and the very positive nature of the projected demand for new innovative telephones persuaded both men that this was the business for them. Their products would integrate the normal function of receiver with those of answerphone, automatic dialling, memory, directory, etc.

It was clear to both men that they had a wonderful start to their enterprises. Few businessmen have the benefit of extensive market information when they decide to start up — most have to base their research on less formal and less expensive techniques. Inward and Smart were fortunate, and both felt confident of what the future would bring.

Each man estimated that the technical research and development would take approximately one year, by which time both companies should be in a position to go into production. They were promised the help and co-operation of the University and they each found a small workshop within the campus for which they paid a nominal rent. They would both require further finance, but for the moment each had enough capital to be getting along with.

Inward set to work, confident that his proven ability as a designer would result in the best possible equipment, technically superb and exactly what all the prospective customers would want. When the design was ready he would raise the necessary finance, employ the required staff, move into the small factory in Snodsville and go into production.

Smart also set to work, but he decided that he would first look up an old colleague, one of the marketing managers at his previous employer, who he knew had been thinking of leaving for some time. His friend, George King, had put by a little capital and Smart offered him a participating directorship with 30% of the equity. King examined the project and quickly decided to join Smart as Marketing Director, gave his notice and started, full-time, three months later.

While Smart was developing the basic design with a secondee from the University, King began work on setting up the company and took a first look at the marketing problems they were about to face. He researched the market for more information and found the results of a consumer attitude survey recently conducted by the Post Office and published only six months earlier. He studied the competition and examined their marketing methods, channels of distribution and prices.

King and Smart met often. They discussed the implications of the findings made by King and the practicality of implementing them. For example: King established that pastel shades were very much more in demand by domestic users of telephone equipment, whilst business users preferred the harder reds and greens and they both hated the traditional grey; the price of similar equipment on the market (all imported) varied considerably; many of the retail outlets would display the products stacked in their cartons; push button dialling was preferred by all users; most successful firms operating in the sector used an advertising led campaign backed by account sales managers and a merchandising team. Some made extensive use of mail order.

As the year progressed Smart and King worked together on a comprehensive business and marketing plan. They budgeted for production, overheads, administrative support and a sensible marketing campaign. They raised the finance with little trouble and moved into their small factory some three months before they planned to go into full production.

Meanwhile, Inward worked hard. He concentrated on perfecting the design and establishing sources of supply for parts of the assembly that his company would not be able to manufacture. He found a plastics firm which would provide the moulded cases — all grey! He ordered brown cardboard cartons with his name and address very neatly printed on the side. And he was most fortunate in finding a keyboard manufacturer who would supply the push-button dialling panels.

Approximately three months before he was due to move into his factory he advertised for staff. Having persuaded his design assistant to join him as Production Director the most important post to fill was that of Sales Director. Here Inward felt himself to be particularly lucky in being able to employ a man of considerable experience; he had sold everything from life insurance to computers. Yes, thought Inward, although Gerald Appleby-Smooth had not actually held a sales management job he could sell fridges to Eskimos, and that was exactly what SEDATE needed.

The respective Managing Directors and their colleagues interviewed many job applicants and they had soon filled all vacancies. Because he had a little extra time, Smart was able to provide a short training course for his production staff and King was able to train his new Marketing Department. Inward would be able to train his people on the job, and Appleby-Smooth did not really see the need for training his salesmen; after all they *were* experienced!

Whizzo's new Production Director had straight away been involved with the regular meetings of King and Smart. He was then able to arrange the supply of suitable components including moulded cases in a range of splendid colours. He also secured a supply of printed cartons in full colour illustrating the product in use and incorporating a powerful sales message. The name Whizzo was very much in evidence and this would do a great deal to support brand indentification when advertising got under way.

Finally, they were both ready to go into production and each Managing Director drew up a company management chart looking like this:

SEDATE Ltd

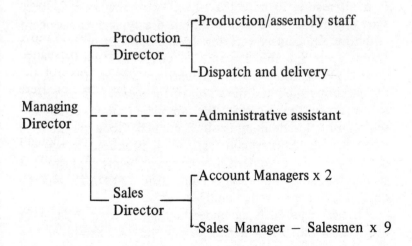

Whizzo Electronics Ltd

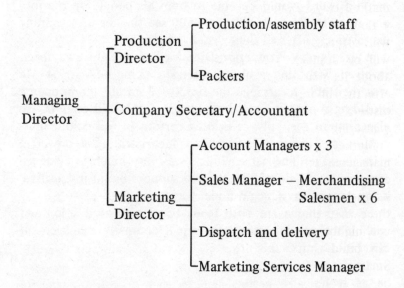

SALES BASED OR MARKETING ORIENTED

It is interesting to note that these two companies, as they start out in life, have each established a typical management structure. Of course, very few businesses start up on such a grand scale but this illustration serves our purpose well.

SEDATE Ltd is very much *sales based*, note the absence of marketing skills and the status of the dispatch department, and works on the principle: 'We can make it; now get out and sell it.' But this thinking is old fashioned. Gone are the days when British industry could sell all it produced to a world of ever growing consumerism. In an age of highly sophisticated communication and intense competition SEDATE will be operating under a severe handicap.

What is required is an understanding of what the market needs, how much it is willing to pay, how it operates and an idea of the most efficient way of reaching that market. Whizzo is streets ahead. Its product, whilst offering perfectly acceptable quality, more accurately fits the needs of the market. Having taken the trouble to find out, Whizzo offers a range of colours suitable for all potential customers; it will offer an appropriate pricing structure; the packaging will be designed with the retailer in mind and it will set about its marketing campaign in a way most relevant and effective in terms of the target market. Whizzo will have a distinct advantage over its local competitor, it is a *marketing oriented* company.

Marketing is a way of approaching business; not only a management function but a method of ensuring that all the company's activities are directed towards the interests of its customers, and do not merely satisfy the aspirations of the owners and staff. SEDATE is production centred; Inward is a highly proficient engineer who knows exactly what he can build, but very little of what his customers require. Smart is also very able and although his product may not be as technically perfect as Inward's, Whizzo telephones will undoubtedly be more successful in the marketplace.

It is vital for any business to plan ahead. Not only for the short term. To be successful a company must have some idea of where it is going in the years to come. This applies especially to new businesses.

Because we are all consumers, we all think that we are expert on the subject of marketing — we feel that we instinctively *know* what our customers will want. But everyone should take the trouble to learn the techniques of marketing and practice its philosophy. It is impossible for a company to market efficiently if no one in the company knows anything about marketing. Likewise, it is pointless for a firm to produce sophisticated marketing plans if the owners, directors and staff do not 'think marketing' and if all the necessary information is not available.

Back in Snodsville, King and Smart set aside one long meeting each month to discuss marketing. They started this back in their planning days and consider these meetings invaluable. Over at SEDATE, the deep commitment of Inward to his design and production together with the arrogance of Appleby-Smooth mean that they never discuss marketing in any constructive way. They occasionally agree to place an advertisement here or send a leaflet there, and Inward did mention once that he thought Appleby-Smooth was, 'a little generous with his discounts.'

Whizzo had developed a standard format for the marketing meetings. Apart from Smart and King, all the managers that were available attended, and once every three months all the sales staff came; on these occasions the meeting went on for most of the day.

Meetings were divided into five sessions: research and information, sales and distribution, advertising and promotion, product policy, and planning. Planning was really a summary of the results of their earlier discussions and here they allocated resources to wherever necessary. All present were involved as much as possible and each was made to feel part of a successful team. This was particularly important to the salesmen who spent much of their time out on the road.

King was aware of the importance of discussing each marketing function in turn. It gave the team the opportunity to tackle each problem, and the discipline meant that they very rarely overlooked an important point. Also, they could get down to the nitty-gritty of the advertising campaign, the new promotional leaflet or revised sales targets in a constructive manner. But it was the planning session that was considered the most important. This gave all present a perspective of the company as a whole, how all their efforts fitted in with the scheme of things and how the correct balance (marketing mix) was to be achieved.

A good example of how successful the meetings were occurred one day when King announced plans to expand the mail order side of the operation. This gave rise, for obvious reasons, to more than a little discontent from the salesmen. It was decided to place a series of advertisements in the Sunday Colour Supplements (this decision was taken on the advice of Whizzo's advertising agency) designed to evoke a direct response to be handled by the company's own dispatch department. But, after some heated discussion, it was agreed that all advertisement copy would include the fact that customers could also purchase the products at certain retail outlets and listed the major stockists. The campaign not only brought in new mail order business, but had the effect of increasing public awareness of Whizzo telephones and consequently sales through the traditional outlets increased considerably. The salesmen were happy, and the directors of Whizzo delighted.

MARKETING IS FOR ALL BUSINESSES

It must not be assumed from the foregoing that the use of effective marketing is confined to manufacturers with over twenty staff. All businesses benefit from a controlled and thoughtful approach to their day to day operations and in particular, their marketing activities. People in services, the one-man band, the retailer and the tradesman should all 'think marketing'.

How often have we experienced:

● the dingy pub with the ill-mannered landlord;
● the insurance man who promises to ring back, but never does;
● the shoddy leaflet that merely persuades one to go elsewhere;
● the badly worded advertisement that omits address and telephone number;
● the pale, spotty and grubby youth serving in the health-food shop;
● the mail order firm with no literature, or
● the non-existent after-sales service?

Attention, awareness and sometimes a little expense would eliminate all of the above problems and in every case improve business.

Marketing is too often made out to be only for the big boys. Perhaps large companies can afford to be highly scientific, and there is no doubt that the professionalism and power shows, but when it comes down to it, marketing is often just good sense. It is putting customers first, establishing their needs and meeting them. The customer *is* always right!

Creative marketing is essential but creating markets must be left to those with the resources. A cohesive and considered approach is the order of the day, and there is no business, large or small, that should not comply.

Finally, let us take a last look at Snodsville and see just where SEDATE went wrong.

Company Structure and Planning

Even down to the name, which is clumsy and projects the wrong image, SEDATE has committed a series of unnecessary breaches of good marketing practice. Inward is a clever engineer but has no concept of the customer, competition or demand. He commits the cardinal sin of assuming that all he has to do is make a product and then it will sell itself. Consequently he is left with a less than ideal product and an inefficient management structure which is incapable of making any integrated marketing plans for the immediate or distant future.

Marketing Research

Whizzo and SEDATE, by having access to the results of the survey commissioned by the University, were given a flying start. Not many businesses have this sort of opportunity and it is probably due solely to this that SEDATE is still in business. But Inward made no attempt to discover more about the market into which he was about to plunge himself and his new company. Informal study and use of previously published information is an inexpensive way of gaining knowledge which may spell the difference between success and failure.

Sales and Distribution

As Inward was soon to find out, there is more to achieving sales than just selling. Of primary importance is to establish the most appropriate method or methods of distribution. Whizzo found that equipment of this type was sold mainly through large multiples (retail chains) although there was some evidence of mail order. Armed with this information King was able to recruit the most suitable sales team and make provision for a mail order operation, with the dispatch under his control.

SEDATE employs a totally inadequate sales force with a team of untrained salesmen headed by a Director hired for his ability as a smooth salesman rather than any flair for organisation. The job they have to do is most difficult and results will be based on luck rather than judgement. A dissatisfied and badly managed sales force is destined for a high staff turnover rate adding more problems to an already strained situation.

Advertising and Sales Promotion

Planning and budgeting is probably more important here than in any other aspect of marketing. Whether it is a national advertising campaign, point-of-sale material, press contact or simple promotional leaflet, effect is maximised by planning, consistency and professionalism.

Because Whizzo had a sensible budget it was able to

obtain the services of a small provincial advertising agency which not only created the material and selected the best media, but helped a lot with the initial planning.

At SEDATE advertisement space was booked on an *ad hoc* basis, whenever the mood struck Inward or Appleby-Smooth, or when they were approached by an enterprising ad. salesman. SEDATE had made no plans for the vital sales literature or any other promotional material and when they do get round to producing any it will almost certainly look rushed and unprofessional.

Product Policy

Here was the most obvious difference between SEDATE and Whizzo. Using the results of their research, Smart and his Production Director were able to produce a range of products designed specifically with the market in mind. The colours (very important with a permanent item in the home or office) were attractive to potential purchasers and Whizzo was sure that the facilities its machines offered were exactly what the customers wanted. Because the product would be displayed in its carton, stacked in retail stores, it was important to design the carton so that it acted as its own point-of-sale promotion. Whizzo telephones would soon be recognised in the stores, and potential customers would be encouraged by a powerful sales message. The pricing structure (including discounts for larger dealers) had been based on real information.

On the other hand SEDATE had none of these benefits. The packaging told the customer nothing, not even what was inside the box, the colour of the equipment would not help sales, and the facilities offered by the machines themselves were only what Inward thought best. SEDATE had no coherent discount policy and the salesmen would get away with what they could. This would eventually lead to aggravation from stockists as some would be able to offer the product at considerably less than others.

In a competitive and challenging world, if a business is to survive and prosper it must reduce the risks it takes. Marketing cannot eliminate the risks inherent in running a business but, like all management, can minimise those risks and provide the route to success. It is likely that Whizzo will face many crises but it is equipped to overcome them. SEDATE, on the other hand, is a very likely candidate to join the ranks of the majority of new business enterprises that fail.

APPROACHING BUSINESS THE MARKETING WAY

CHECKLIST

1. Does your company have an executive, at Director level, with the specific task of marketing?

2. Have all your senior management (including yourself) an understanding of the principles of marketing?

3. Do you have a written marketing plan for
   a) the current year?
   b) the next 3 years?
   c) the next 5 years?

4. Have you made a positive attempt to identify your customers, and have you *adjusted* your policy to accommodate their needs?

5. Do you 'think marketing' and have you told your staff to think of the customers first?

6. Do you regularly train your selling and other marketing staff?

2
The Marketing Mix

Unless business owners and managers are prepared to accept that their customers are number one priority and to take a marketing approach to business management, they will never obtain the full benefits available through effective marketing. There is no magic! Effective marketing is not beyond any business practitioners if they first tackle the principles and then consider the implications of every decision.

The marketing mix is a complex of decisions making up the public and private profile of a business. Each decision must be rooted in technical competence, but merit alone is not enough — bringing/all the elements together into a cohesive and effective strategy is the secret of success. This strategy, which manifests itself in annual and longer term marketing plans, is unique to the business, its customers and products or services, and determines its eventual position in the market-place.

The relationships between the elements of the marketing mix are intricate. Although we may examine them independently, it must be remembered that the elements do not act in isolation; the implementation of any marketing activity will affect many other aspects of the business. For example: any benefit of a change in packaging design will be lost if not reinforced by new promotional support, but first it must be researched; a new pricing policy will affect salemen's commission and the profits made by distributors. Comprehensive planning will minimise the risks of embarrassing repercussions from changes in marketing policy — but first we must understand what makes up the marketing mix.

MARKETING RESEARCH

Running a business without the benefit of marketing information is akin to driving a car blindfold; although highly dangerous it *is* possible to reach one's destination, but nobody in their right mind would attempt this as a form of transport. For exactly the same reasons no one should even consider managing a business blindfold.

Marketing research is the means by which the information necessary to run a business is obtained and the way that knowledge may then be used in constructive management. Every company, no matter what its size, must research its market, customers and competition; first to set it on the right course and then continually to monitor its performance. A retailer depending on passing trade needs to discover pedestrian levels at alternative sites, an hotel should discover if its service satisfies its guests and the soft toy manufacturer ought to find out if people really want purple teddy bears!

As we have said, marketing is a way of approaching business and is concerned with all the activities involved in moving a product or service from the producer to the end consumer (the right product or service). It follows that marketing research should be concerned with the collection and use of information that will help the business owner and managers make better decisions on *all* aspects of their marketing activities. For this reason, marketing research is at the heart of every marketing plan. There is no point constructing an elaborate strategy if it is based on guesswork and ignorance.

But facts are not that difficult to find, it is a relatively simple matter to ask a few questions, it is asking the right questions in the right way that is the difficult part. Similarly, there is no shortage of marketing information published by a great many agencies that make information their business. Every firm has a rich supply of information contained within its own records. Again, it is obtaining useful data, separating the wheat from the chaff, that is the problem, and then applying the new knowledge to the problems in hand.

There is no point in equipping yourself with masses of facts and figures, analysing them and studying them if you are not going to use them. Objectives must be established; all research should be done for a reason and the results must appear in some tangible form. Decision making is made both easier and more effective if the evidence is based on fact and is presented in such a way as to eliminate misinterpretation. Marketing research will never replace entrepreneurial flair, but if used together the two make a formidable team.

SALES AND DISTRIBUTION

A company may produce the very best product known to man, it may offer the very latest in fashion or invent the ultimate labour-saving device, but there is no point whatsoever in any of this activity if the product or service is never sold. It is the purpose of the sales and distribution function to see to it that customers are found and persuaded to buy, and that they have a supply of the product or service *when they need it*. It is only when goods and services are actually exchanged for money that a firm sees any return on its investment.

This all seems rather obvious, but surprisingly there are many businesses that fail to recognise the significance of effective selling, and even more that fail to ensure adequate distribution of their goods and services. Every time a retailer is asked for an item which is out of stock it is a sale lost to him, the wholesaler, the agent (if there is one) and the manufacturer. Every time a householder, in frustration at not being able to find anyone to do a job, does it himself, it is a lost sale. And every time a business cancels an order for supplies, or goes elsewhere because of inadequate service, it is a sale lost (a sale that may all too often go overseas).

With the exception of unusual cases, notably mail order, in every business somebody has to sell personally. This may involve selling direct to the user as in the case of most services and many industrial products, or selling to an intermediary such as a wholesaler or department store buyer. Every business owner should ask himself: Who does the selling? If there is no immediate answer he had better get on to it; contrary to popular belief, customers do not beat a path to every business door!

Many businesses will employ salesmen and the business owner or manager will have to ensure they are properly managed, a perennial problem that calls for great care and attention. In terms of personal relations salesmen are often difficult to deal with, they are by nature independently minded and require careful handling and constant motivation. Sales management is all about organisation; territories, efficient routeing and good reporting bring results and somebody must be responsible.

Distribution means much more than transportation to the marketer. There are set channels of distribution for certain types of businesses; it would be very difficult for a market gardener to sell asparagus direct to the end consumer who would normally buy from a retailer. But the vegetables will first have to go to market and then possibly to a wholesaler before they reach the retailer. Alternatively, the market gardener may sell his produce to a canning or freezing processor, a soup manufacturer or even open up a farm shop to sell part of his output. Clearly the producer has a choice as to the best method of distribution and on this decision will depend packaging, promotion, selling and pricing policies.

Manufacturers and businesses operating the channels of distribution must ensure that all potential customers have access to their products, and this means careful control and maintenance of supplies. Asparagus will soon rot if left unsold due to over-supply; under-supply will result in lost sales. Retailers play a vital role in this marketing process and their stockholding policies affect most manufacturers and producers. But retailers are businesses in their own right and will benefit from the implementation of good marketing practice.

The function of sales and distribution is often considered the 'sharp end' of the marketing mix. This very fact makes it essential that its execution is honed to a fine point. Profits can only be generated if sales are made — enough sales at the right price.

ADVERTISING AND SALES PROMOTION

The purpose of advertising and sales promotion is to persuade customers, including industrial users and those operating the channels of distribution, to adopt a favourable attitude to an organisation and its products or services. From the humble leaflet, through editorial comment, to the large advertisement in a Sunday colour supplement, techniques are designed to inform, tempt, persuade and create images.

Nowhere in his armoury does the marketer have a wider selection of techniques than in advertising and sales promotion; a vast range often collectively known as indirect selling. Paid advertising, or 'above the line' promotion, is a familiar part of all our lives as are the special offers, promotional leaflets and display material which are all 'below the line' techniques. Most smaller firms use the mail to promote business, a medium that can bring excellent results if used properly.

In some cases, the buying decision is actually triggered by indirect means – the special offer leaflet pushed through a customer's door or the advertisement selling incontinence aids by mail order. More usually, advertising and sales promotion techniques are used to reinforce the sales process; to inform and to generate a feeling of trust in the company and what it has to offer. Much advertising only attempts to achieve changes in attitude and some campaigns seem very obtuse. Few would consider that a tiger loping across the sands has very much to do with selling Esso petrol, but it does give the feeling of power and as such helps to mould attitudes.

All businesses are engaged in some form of indirect selling. Every single piece of paper generated by a business is a reflection of that business: letter, leaflet, menu, catalogue or price list. Advertisements appear in their millions in local, national and trade media and, whatever the critics say, provide an essential service for both buyer and seller. But whichever technique, or techniques used, the business owner must ensure that he says exactly what he means and that the material is carefully produced. Businesses should be constantly aware of their relationships with the public; using the press, dealing with enquiries and looking after their employees in an endless effort to promote good will.

Consistency and *professionalism* are the keys to effective indirect selling. A business representing itself as bright and modern through its product and advertising will only confuse its customers if its literature is typeset in Old English Palace Script. How is it that some mints are 'as cold as ice' and others the 'hottest thing in sweets'? Because of a consistent and professional campaign putting over a message to a receptive audience.

The smaller business may not be able to create markets or shape attitudes in the same way as the multi-nationals. But it can promote itself in a way that will capture the confidence of customers and increase its business. Nothing is worse than poorly presented promotional material; badly written, badly illustrated and only convincing potential customers that this business is one to be avoided at all costs.

As with all marketing activities, the need for planning and budgeting is paramount in good indirect selling. Planning should ensure that promotional effort is reinforcing other parts of the marketing mix — not contradicting them. Indirect selling, if not directed in the right way, may soon lead to a great deal of wasted expenditure. The last thing a small business can afford is the inefficient use of its limited resources.

INDIRECT v DIRECT — THE PRODUCT GROUPS

The most delicate balance within the marketing mix is usually that between direct selling effort and indirect; whether to concentrate on pulling in sales through personal contact or pushing sales through advertising and sales promotion. Most businesses operate with a combination of both — the emphasis depends largely on the product or service in question. A simple guide is to examine the major product groups and decide in which area your product or service lies.

Consumer Consumables	Consumer Durables
Industrial Consumables	Industrial Durables

Although this should only be considered a rough rule of thumb this analysis should help the business owner or manager to see if his major marketing effort is directed in the right way.

a) Consumer goods and services tend to be pushed through indirect means whilst Industrials are pulled through direct selling.

b) Durables tend to require more direct sales effort and Consumables more indirect support.

So, fast moving consumer goods (fmcg) such as cornflakes, meals in restaurants, alcoholic drinks, tobacco products, etc. will be heavily marketed through indirect means; machine tools, plant, office cleaning contracts and other industrial durables cannot be marketed without substantial direct sales effort. The other two groups: consumer durables; double glazing, insurance, washing machines, cars, and industrial consumables; stationery, nuts and bolts, printing and cartons, are examples: will be marketed using a combination of indirect and direct means with the emphasis on an all-round effort.

PRODUCT POLICY

It is often said that product management has no place in the realms of small business marketing strategy. True, large consumer manufacturers operate a policy of product development that few small firms could emulate. Unilever, Rowntree, Heinz and other such giants employ armies of brand and product staff whose sole purpose is to look after product marketing. They work with advertising agencies, packaging designers, PR consultants and promotions experts to develop brand indentities and push their products into the homes of millions of consumers.

Although a small firm could not hope to match the sophistication of the big boys, a carefully planned and monitored marketing approach to business will help ensure a firm gets the most from its products and services and is selling them at the right prices. Conditions in the market-place are rarely static for long; every product and service has a life cycle and if a firm is to stay on top it must continually re-assess and develop its product policy.

A word about *services*. For the purposes of product management and most other marketing considerations, services should be treated in exactly the same way as products. Excellent examples may be found in the world of franchising; Dyno-Rod, the drain cleaners and Prontaprint instant print shops have put in a great deal of effort to develop their services. Few would dispute that Prontaprint has a highly visible brand identity supported by a 'package' based on the very best marketing principles. Services have all the characteristics of products (in marketing terms) and businesses in the service sector, from window cleaners to entertainers, will benefit from following the basics of good product management.

Few businesses operate with only one product selling at a single price; the most effective firms have a well balanced range. The success of this *product mix* depends on the continuous development of new products and the regular elimination of weak ones. Product decisions must be based on sound marketing research but depend on the preparedness of business owners and managers to effect change. Few decisions are harder than to drop a product that has served a company well but has come to the end of its useful life.

The importance of packaging is often overlooked by the smaller business where cost and availability of suitable materials take on great significance. It is more difficult for a small firm to arrange a one-off moulding for plastic containers or demand a special make of cardboard cartons — some firms have to make the best of standard items. In response to growing consumer sophistication, technology has provided a dazzling array of packaging materials and processes and the choice open to the business owner and manager is wide. Practical considerations are important but do not necessarily help to build sales — the product and its package are often the most effective promotional tool.

Probably the single most difficult task that a small business owner will face is pricing his product or service. This must be seen as a marketing problem and can present a particularly irksome and complex one for the new business with a new product or service. The basic decision is whether the firm intends to skim the market (go for limited sales by creaming off the most attractive propositions) or go for real penetration of the market or a geographical sector of it. There must be provision for costs and a minimum level of profits, but the final decision will depend on that magic factor — enterprise! It is usually a matter of emphasis, but getting it right is guaranteed to keep even the best sleepers awake at night.

Business management is classically divided into four major elements: production, finance, personnel and marketing. It is unlikely that in a small firm these functions are performed by different people, and with the very small business the Managing Director or Proprietor will deal with all of them. Similarly we have seen that the marketing mix comprises four distinct but inter-related elements: research, sales and distribution, advertising and sales promotion, and product policy.

It is unusual for a smaller business to have the resources to employ a manager with the sole responsibility for each function. This makes it vital for the business owner to ensure each element of the mix is catered for and applied with a level of competence. The essence of effective marketing is, having dealt with each and every aspect of the mix, to bring them together in an integrated approach, carefully planned and monitored. In this respect the small firm structure may offer advantages and it is up to the owner to ensure that his firm makes the best of them.

THE MARKETING MIX

CHECKLIST

1. Do you make a conscious effort to research and provide background information for every major marketing decision?

2. Have you identified each major element of the marketing mix and examined how together they affect your business?

3. Have specific measures been taken to ensure integration between each marketing function?

4. Is all your marketing effort based on a consistent theme, and does each activity reinforce this theme?

5. Within which product group does your company's business lie?

6. Do you place emphasis on indirect or direct selling, and is this in line with other businesses in your group?

7. Have you tried altering this emphasis and considered the implications of doing so?

8. Have you tested different methods of advertising and sales promotion and carefully monitored the results?

9. Does your product mix allow for unexpected product failures?

10. Are you constantly seeking new product ideas?

11. Is your intention to skim the market or to penetrate, and does your pricing and other marketing policy reflect this?

PART II
Marketing Research

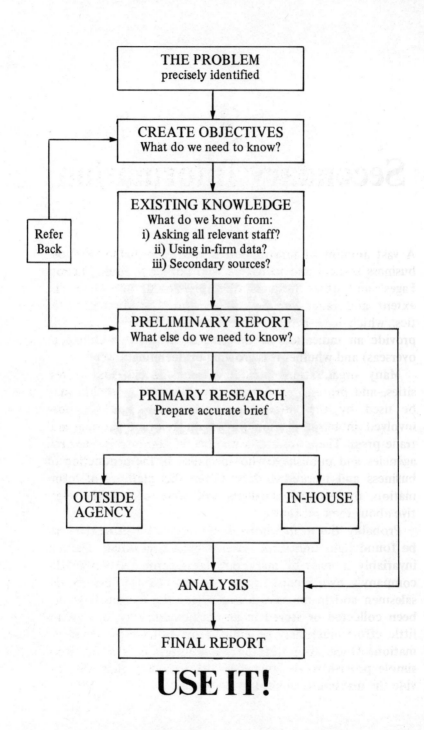

3
Secondary Information

A vast amount of information is readily available for those business owners and managers who bother to look. 'Yellow Pages' and other business directories will soon show the extent and range of the competition. Government statistics, which have been greatly improved in recent years, will provide an indication of the size of the market (home or overseas) and whether it is growing or declining.

Many organisations including trade associations, universities, and professional institutes publish material that may be used by the enterprising businessman, and all those involved in business should read the relevant national and trade press. There are also a number of commercial research agencies and publishers who specialise in the production of business and marketing data. Given this plethora of information, owners and managers will need to be fairly selective about their reading.

Probably the most under-used source of information can be found right under the nose of the businessman. There is invariably a mass of marketing facts contained within the company's own records, most obviously those held by the salesmen and in the sales office. Often the records have not been collected or stored in any systematic way, but with a little effort much may be gained from full use of this information. Once aware of the possibilities, it is a relatively simple process to design paperwork in a way that will provide the maximum amount of usable data.

Retailers and other distributive firms, by necessity, maintain extensive records which can often be used to much better effect. Stock control records, for example, contain a considerable amount of market intelligence if analysed properly. Hotels, restaurants and other businesses in the service sector may, by examining their customer records, establish the nature of their market, trends, the effect of price changes, and monitor the general efficiency of their operation.

The greater availability of micro-computers should make the whole process of secondary marketing research an almost automatic part of the everyday operation of the smaller business. Never before have there been more sources of information available to the businessman, nor organisations ready and willing to help. Information is the life blood of good decision-making, and making the right decision can be the difference between success and failure for the smaller business.

IN-COMPANY INFORMATION SYSTEMS

Every self respecting large and medium-sized company has an internal *marketing information system*. Normally computer based, these systems are fed with a whole range of relevant marketing information and, in return, issue on a weekly and monthly basis a picture of the company's position for use by everyone taking marketing decisions. These systems vary in sophistication but (should) always provide sufficient information to drastically reduce the risks of decision making. And that is what marketing research is all about — the reduction of risk by providing the best possible terms of reference on which to base decisions.

For the smaller business owner or manager, what is particularly interesting about these sophisticated information systems is not what they produce but what goes into them. It takes a clever computer programmer to devise a good output, but it takes a systematic approach to data collection to provide the computer system with the right material to start with. And there is no reason for any business not to use the wealth of information it has to aid better decision making.

Smaller business owners and managers should set up marketing information systems, if they have a micro-computer available all the better, if not it will mean a little extra work, but it will be well worth the effort. All businesses are awash with information − orders, invoices sent out, invoices paid, salesmen's call reports, complaints/ returns, bills paid, stock purchases, stock-holding, customer profiles and details of competitors. Unfortunately, in many firms this information, once it is used for its original purpose, gets filed away and lost forever. A good information system starts by presenting all data in a way that will make future processing possible and then by routinely collecting that data.

For example, a salesman's call report will have a list of the calls made on a day by day basis. But it should also indicate the purpose of the call and a reference to his contact cards will show the type and size of each customer. This information can then be used to establish contact/ sales ratios and guide the sales manager in his control and planning activities (see Chapter 6).

An effective marketing information system can only become a reality, therefore, if *all* incoming data is *first* presented in a form that allows analysis and is then *collected systematically* as it comes in. Once information has been filed, even over a fairly short period of time, it becomes an impossible task to retrieve it. There must be a continuous collection of data. To facilitate this procedure, forms must be designed, not only with day-to-day uses in mind, but with due consideration to the provision of data into the information system. Data must be broken down as much as possible into its component parts, disaggregated.

Expenditures must be allocated to specific budgets – right
from the start, and sales must be recorded product by product, by price and by territory – right from the start.

In-company information may be conveniently divided
into two distinct categories – operational and sales. The
smaller business will find that effective use of data is the
cheapest and most useful of all marketing research activities.
But a positive approach is necessary as the system has to
be established right the way through the day to day activity
of running the business. First decide what is wanted from the
system, and what is possible, and then set up the machinery.

OPERATIONAL DATA

Operational data is essentially financial information without
which no business can judge its profitability nor its efficiency.
There is absolutely no point in running a business if it doesn't
make a profit and it is too late if you can only establish the
business has been running at a loss when the annual accounts
are prepared. The business owner or manager must be able to
monitor performance as it goes along, and it is the responsibility of effective marketing to make sure that the business
is operating efficiently and at a profit.

The major financial tool of the smaller business operator
is the profit and loss account. Not the annual one prepared
by the firm's accountant, but an operational version showing
exactly how the business is faring month by month. (An
extension of this, the budgeted cash flow, is the primary
financial and marketing planning tool and is discussed in
Chapter 14.) The marketer's profit and loss account should
be designed to give much more than a statement of financial
affairs and will provide all the operating indicators on a
monthly basis.

				Operating Ratios
Sales (net of returns)			50,000	100%
Opening stock	40,000			
Purchases	26,000			
Direct expenses	5,000	71,000		
Less closing stock		41,000		
Cost of goods sold			30,000	60%
Gross Profit			20,000	40%
Overheads			5,000	10%
Marketing expenses				
Sales salaries and commissions	4,600			
Advertising and promotion	2,000			
Administration	500			
Other	400			
Total			7,500	15%
Net Profit			7,500	15%

Fig 3.1. An example of a simple profit and loss account showing the key operating ratios.

The profit and loss example shown in Fig 3.1 is a very simple one. In practice the monthly operational account will include a lot more information and will be structured to suit the type of business. Budgets for sales and expenditure will normally be shown so a direct comparison between plan and reality may easily be made. If the business has several main products or product groups, each will be taken individually and their contribution to overall gross profits may be established. Similarly, if a business operates a number of different activities these will be taken one at a time.

Most importantly the account will include a 'year to date' column which provides the most useful guide to how the business is performing by reducing the effects of monthly fluctuations. The annual account will give a full picture of budgeted performance.

The *gross profit ratio* is the difference between cost of sales and value of sales expressed as a percentage of net sales. Cost of sales varies from business to business, a manufacturer would include all production costs while a retailer includes expenses to do with stock handling and storage. But this ratio is a key indicator in terms of pricing purchasing activities. If the ratio is decreasing then the business owner or manager will have to consider a price increase, a more aggressive buying policy or look at the possibility of introducing new product lines that produce greater margins.

A ratio not shown in Fig 3.1, the *sales returns ratio*, is very important to certain types of business, publishing for example. It is the percentage of gross sales lost against net sales. A high or increasing ratio may indicate faulty production or perhaps bad merchandising, overselling or failure to meet customer expectation.

Expense ratios can be divided into groups such as marketing and overheads and will vary considerably from business to business, even those operating in the same trade. These indicators do, however, show up bad and wasteful policies and if the ratios are not static they may be indicating that a certain activity is losing its effect and mean that a re-assessment is urgently required.

The 'bottom line' for the business owner is the *net profit ratio*. If this is too low it may mean that it's time to sell up and put the capital into a building society. On its own, the net profitability of a business is not a particularly useful indicator as to what is going wrong (or right) with the business. But if the net profit ratio is decreasing it is time to look very closely at the other ratios to see if the problems can be pinpointed.

There are a number of other business ratios that should be used in the course of decision taking. The *mark-up* and *mark-down* ratios are of particular value to retailers and other 'dealers'. A comparison of the mark-up of different products will indicate where the strengths and weaknesses are and which parts of the business should be developed. But products do not always sell at the original selling price, if they don't, then a mark-down ratio (the difference between the original selling price and the actual one) should be established. If there is a consistent pattern to high mark-down ratios on a range of products this will indicate a problem with pricing policy. Low mark-down ratios, on the other hand, indicate effective buying, realistic pricing and good selling.

Stock turnround rate is the number of times the stock turns round in a specified period, usually a year. This rate plays a vital part in measuring the efficiency of buying and selling policy. Big supermarkets operate on incredibly low gross and net profit margins and rely on turning their stocks over many times in order to make a realistic income. The rate can be based either on sales and selling price or on cost prices and is calculated by dividing the total sales (at selling prices or cost prices) by average value of the stock (at selling prices or cost).

SALES DATA

A sales invoice, in its basic form, gives the customer's name and address and shows how much is owed. But with a little thought and planning this simple document can become one of the most useful aids to marketing research. Again, it should be stressed that this transformation can only take place if the form itself is designed to provide all the relevant data; it is no use digging out all the old invoices, it would cost too much even if they contained the right data.

The well designed invoice will show: the customer — name, location, type code and contact; the sale — product by product, prices, discounts, quantities and method of sale; the date. This information, on analysis, can provide sales performance by product line, type of customer, market area and marketing methods. It can give feedback on pricing policy and sales force performance, and it can indicate seasonal trends and product obsolescence.

If the business owner or manager provides himself with an analysis of all these details once a month, and this means extracting all the necessary information *as it comes in*, he will be able to spot weaknesses and strengths in the firm's marketing operation. An analysis of sales compared to targets will soon highlight the ace salesman and the one who is moonlighting, compared product by product trends can soon be spotted and prompt action taken.

The other major source of sales data comes from the records kept by the salesmen and sales managers. Chapter 6 explains in detail how the sales manager (who is quite likely to be the proprietor or managing director of a smaller business) can control sales activity only with the help of well prepared sales information. This set of monthly records will of course be integrated into the marketing information system which has now become a pretty powerful tool of indispensable value to every business.

EXTERNAL SOURCES OF SECONDARY INFORMATION

Marketing intelligence from external sources can provide much useful information as regular input to your marketing information system, and the sources should always be used as the first step in *ad hoc* marketing research projects. The flow chart at the beginning of this chapter shows the role that secondary sources play in the research process. For smaller businesses which do not generally have the time nor the resources to undertake major primary research projects, the use of secondary data becomes all the more important.

Systematic monitoring of the most important sources –

business and trade press, local directories and newspapers and industry statistics — will keep the business owner or manager informed of trends in his industry, movement of competitors and new marketing and technological developments. The use of a press cutting service is useful for some businesses that operate in very wide markets, for others it pays to subscribe to a market intelligence agency such as A. C. Neilsen while other trades are well served by an active Trade Association. Whatever the case, it is vital to keep informed on a regular and routine basis.

Research projects require a different approach to the regular gathering of data. If the business owner or manager is faced with a particular problem he requires very specific information, some or all of it available from secondary sources. The biggest danger is that the general nature of secondary information may mean that it is not exactly relevant to the problem in hand and care must be taken in the application of this data. Sometimes the researcher will strike lucky and find exactly what he wants, other times the data will have to be used as background supportive information, putting some primary research into context or helping the researcher to identify his problem more clearly.

But whatever the problem the golden rule is to try secondary sources first. There are a number of excellent business libraries in the major cities, and most public libraries have a good selection of business directories and other publications. Some trade associations have good libraries and information services and there are many commercial organisations that are in the business of selling information. Every week there are dozens of reports published containing marketing information on a myriad of trades and industries. A number of other bodies provide information of specific use to businesses — Institute of Marketing, Market Research Society and many government organisations should be approached.

GOVERNMENT SOURCES

The Department of Trade at 1 Victoria Street in London is a major supplier of business statistics. The *Business Monitor* series gives details of market size and trends of many areas of business and is published quarterly. Also published by the Department is the monthly magazine *British Business* which contains a mass of useful information including regular lists of other government information when it becomes available.

The British Overseas Trade Board operates as an independent body within the Department of Trade and it publishes many useful items for the exporter or potential exporter. It can provide market intelligence for just about every foreign country and, as well as giving specific guidance to British businesses, can help them find agents and exhibit in overseas markets.

Statistical information abounds on the shelves of Her Majesty's Stationery Office (HMSO) and although much of it is available in libraries, the businessman can purchase published material from the HMSO shops in the major cities. The *Annual Abstract of Statistics* and *Monthly Digest of Statistics* contain information collected by a number of government departments and are always the place to start. The *Censuses* of *Population, Distribution* and *Production* give very detailed information on their respective spheres of interest, and there are masses of regular economic and trade statistics published showing figures and trends. For those that don't know where to start there is a publication *Government Statistics: A Brief Guide to Sources.*

International statistics are produced by a number of bodies, the European Economic Community now produces a large range of information with regular publications and *ad hoc* production of reports. The United Nations regularly publish world statistics and in each country the governments produce published information, but very few places have a service as good as the U.K.

MARKETING INFORMATION

There are a number of bodies that deal specifically with marketing information: The Institute of Marketing, Market Research Society, Industrial Market Research Society, Advertising Association, the Incorporated Society of British Advertisers, the Institute of Practitioners in Advertising and the Institute of Public Relations. All these bodies have some form of information service and all regularly publish very useful material such as the Institute of Marketing's weekly publication *Marketing*. A comprehensive list of all U.K. newspapers and periodicals and their advertising rates can be found in *British Rate and Data* (Brad). Brad also publishes a guide to all the advertising agencies and *Hollis Press and Public Relations Annual* lists all registered public relations consultants. There are other similar press guides published by Benn's and Willings. Audits of Great Britain provides a mass of information on radio and television, and many advertising agencies publish useful data.

COMMERCIAL SOURCES

More general business and market information is available on such a scale that to list all sources would take up several volumes. The best place to start for information on specific industries is probably to refer to *The Directory of Directories* and the *Directory of British Associations*, both published by CBD Research, the contents of which are self-explanatory. Other prolific providers of market intelligence include, Extel Statistical Services, A.C. Nielsen, the Economist Intelligence Unit, AGB Research, Dun and Bradstreet, Institute of Export, Institute of Directors, British Institute of Management, IPC's Marketing Manuals, the Confederation of British Industry, Financial Times, The Times, the Stock Exchange, the clearing banks, merchant banks, stockbrokers, Chambers of Commerce and Trade, Embassies and Consulates, and many more. The important thing to do is to define the objectives of the intended research clearly before entering this mine of information.

SECONDARY SOURCES OF INFORMATION

CHECKLIST

1 Do you use all the marketing information available in your business to minimise risks in decision marking?

2 Have you established a formal marketing information system?

3 Do you consider information needs when you design your company's paperwork?

4 Do you provide yourself with a monthly operational profit and loss account with 'year to date' entries and budgets?

5 Are you aware of the operating ratios in your company and can they be improved?

6 Do you maintain effective monthly sales analysis records?

7 Do you know which is your trade association and are you a member?

8 Can you list all trade publications relevant to your business?

9 Do you make a conscious effort to keep informed of events in your industry and locality?

10 If you have a marketing research problem do you always use secondary sources of information first?

11 Can you list all relevant directories and publishers of information relating to your industry?

4
Primary Research

On many occasions information that a business owner requires will be found from the study of in-firm data or other secondary sources, however, for many purposes it will be necessary to conduct some type of primary investigation. Business owners and managers should always use secondary methods first, they are invariably cheaper, but the information is not always available. Primary research simply means the collection of information for the first time and for a specific purpose; it is usually obtained directly from customers, competitors (not always easy), retailers and wholesalers, or the public at large.

Techniques vary considerably, but need not be anything more than systematically keeping one's nose to the ground and asking questions such as: Who is the competition? What are competitors doing? What prices are they charging and what discount structure do they use? Are my customers happy? Is my advertising bringing in enough response? Is there anything else I should be doing to promote my product or service? The answers to these questions will provide a great deal of invaluable information.

Mention market research to most people and they will immediately think of BBC audience surveys or pretty girls with clip boards. Market research is the study of the events occurring in a market and as such is a specific element within the overall activity of marketing research. It usually refers to some type of primary survey and it is therefore useful to restrict the use of the expression to that function.

Market research does not necessarily involve the use of highly expensive national surveys — which is fortunate as the smaller business cannot usually afford them. By questioning a pre-determined cross section (known as a sample) of customers, past and present, a business owner can soon get an idea of how his product or service is received and perhaps, how it may be improved.

Often, a trade association will sponsor a market survey for its members or a group of businesses may pool their resources and commission a survey for themselves. Surveys may be based on interviews or questionnaires or both and will almost always use only a sample of the total population or universe. (Population and universe are statistical expressions meaning all those people or firms that make up a certain category, e.g. customers, women in Wales, teenagers in Milton Keynes, etc).

Primary research should not be considered the sole domain of the large consumer companies although they use it a lot to great effect. A sensible approach to fact finding will reveal much valuable data with which the managers of a business may improve their understanding of the various marketing problems they face. There is no doubt that effective marketing research can greatly aid the development of the smaller business.

WHAT QUESTIONS?

Whilst it would probably be an exaggeration to say that managing a business involves lurching from crisis to crisis, it is certainly true that the business owner or manager moves from problem to problem of which each needs a solution. Setting up an effective marketing information system will help provide better terms of reference for the decision maker, and often a little *ad hoc* secondary research is enough to guide the way to a solution. But there will be occasions when this information is just not enough and the business owner or manager will have to look further for an answer.

Primary research is sometimes the only way to discover how to tackle a problem, and when this happens it helps to know where to start. Although marketing research is a relatively new activity, starting in the 1930s in the U.S., it is now such a powerful force that no large consumer company will make a major marketing decision without the benefit of substantial researched information. Our lives are greatly affected by primary marketing research. Fashions, pop songs, radio and television programmes are all the result of highly researched decisions.

The smaller business owner or manager must not feel intimidated by the vast sums of money spent on research, but he must recognise that in his own way he needs it just as much as the big boys. We are simply talking about reducing risks by providing relevant information through collecting facts, analysing them and applying the results to help solve a particular problem. And that is the key — once a problem has been identified and the need for further information established, the project must be perfectly defined and absolutely clear. Whether the research is to be carried out by the owner or manager himself or given to an agency, the terms of reference must be thought out thoroughly and written down lucidly.

The range of possible questions that can be asked through marketing research is very broad. Research can collect facts, examine people's attitudes and opinions, and test marketing activities. It records, analyses, interprets and reports, but never actually makes a decision — that is left to the decision maker, the business owner or manager. The job of research, secondary and primary, is to better equip the decision maker; not do his job for him.

Fig 4.1 Major marketing questions for the smaller business

The Market	● What is its size by volume and value? ● What are the trends and what outside factors are influencing them? ● How is it structured — by industry, by geography and by customers? ● What is our market share and who are our competitors? ● Where are the most promising overseas markets and what are their characteristics?
The Customer	● Who buys our products or services — sex, age, class, income group? ● Where do they live? ● How much and how often do they buy? ● What are people's needs in relation to our product or service? ● What are customers' attitudes towards our company and its products and services?
Products and Services	● Is the quality satisfactory? ● Does it have all the necessary features? ● Are we selling at the right price? ● How are our products or services used? ● Where do our products or services stand in relation to their direct competitors? ● What is the market potential of a particular new product or service? ● What results do we want from a test market? ● Are any of our products or services obsolete or nearing the end of their lives?
Marketing Activities	● Is our distribution set-up adequate to meet market requirements? ● Is there a better, more efficient way to distribute our products or services? ● How effective is our advertising and sales promotional efforts? ● Is our direct sales effort all it should be and how does each part compare with the rest? ● Do we provide adequate customer service? ● What is our corporate image and does it reflect our plans?
Company Organisation	● What is the potential of a particular new site? ● Should we make this business acquisition?

The list of questions shown in Fig 4.1 gives an indication of the range of problems that may be tackled through marketing research. It is not intended to be fully comprehensive but does give an idea of the scope of questions that the smaller business owner or manager should be asking himself. When considering a research project a standard sequence should be followed and the following guide should be used in conjunction with the flow chart shown at the beginning of Chapter 3.

1 Define the problem clearly and lucidly.

2 Set objectives and establish exactly what information is needed from the research.

3 Decide what method or methods to be used (always use secondary sources of information first). Choice is from: formal or structured interview with questionnaire, personal or telephone; questionnaire through the post; informal interviews — personal or telephone; or observation.

4 Will it be necessary to use a sample? If so how should it be structured?

5 Construction of questionnaire or interview guide.

6 Analysis of results.

7 Report and application of findings.

Once the need for primary research is established, one immediate option is to approach a research agency. This is normally very expensive but offers the great advantage that the work is going to be substantially better than if the business (without its own professional marketing research research department) does the work itself. However, for the smaller business, unless the project is of major significance, the use of an agency is not a practical proposition.

There is one exception: there is a growth in the use of 'piggy-back' or omnibus research. Here, an agency announces that it is researching a particular population, for example 12-15 year-old girls, grocery independents, OAPs in Derbyshire, etc. It will construct a significant sample and put the questionnaire on the market. Any organisation that wishes to question the sample may have a question included. The agency will help structure the questions, and a small business may benefit from professional primary research at a fraction of the cost of an entire project.

If an agency is used in any way the prime consideration of the business owner or manager is to provide a precise brief. The agency will assist in establishing the best way of obtaining the information required, prepare questionnaires, design samples and produce reports, but it is the client, and the client alone, that knows what questions need answers. An incomplete or misleading brief may well end in a brilliant piece of research on the wrong subject, irrelevant to the project, and a complete waste of time and money.

METHODS OF PRIMARY RESEARCH

The most widely used method of research is the questionnaire; sent by post, left in the hotel bedroom, filled in with an order form, or completed by an interviewer over the telephone or at a face-to-face interview. The most obvious group at which to direct questions is customers and it is probably true to say that more may be gained from a formal approach to customers than any other single method of research.

Post, telephone or personal
Each method of approaching an interviewee has its advantages and disadvantages. When customers spend some time on the premises such as in hotels, restaurants and private hospitals, it is relatively simple to ask them a few questions

(not so easy to get significant answers) and the problem of how is more or less solved. But with the exception of these cases a decision has to be made on the basis of cost versus quality and quantity of information required.

The personal interview has the greatest advantage of bringing flexibility and control and allows far more detailed information to be collected. Also, if the nature of the survey is complex, or a sample of a product needs to be seen to be understood, the personal interview is the only method. On the other hand, personal interviewing is expensive and time consuming. The smaller business owner or manager is not likely to be able to spare the time for a personal interview survey but there are freelance skilled interviewers that may be hired on a project basis.

The advantages of using the telephone, especially for fairly localised surveys are great. It is more flexible than a postal survey and the response rate is considerably higher. Often people can be contacted by telephone that would not grant a personal interview and would not answer a mailed questionnaire. It is also a very fast method and the smaller business owner or manager could probably conduct a limited telephone survey himself. The disadvantages are: that the respondent has little time to think and will sometimes say things which aren't exactly accurate; only a limited amount of information may be collected; and if the survey is on a national or international basis, the telephone will be prohibitively expensive.

Using a mailed questionnaire is the cheapest of all methods, especially if sent with another piece of correspondence that would have been sent anyway. Respondents have time to think about their answers and some people will respond that would not normally express their feelings on a personal basis. A mailed questionnaire is very objective and can be made anonymous. But the disadvantages are great: there is a notoriously low rate of response and it is difficult to determine whether the response is representative and the answers valid; only a limited amount of information may be gained and there is no flexibility at all.

The questionnaire

Whichever of the above methods are selected a questionnaire is required. Unless the object of the research is of an open-ended nature and an informal interview is used, the interviewer must follow a set pattern and stick to the questions. A questionnaire for a personal or telephone interview will look physically different from one sent in the post or given to a customer to fill in, but the principles of question construction remain the same.

An example of an actual questionnaire prepared by a respected marketing research agency is shown in Fig 4.2. Questions must be constructed to provide the information required and to remove any possibility of ambiguity or misunderstanding. They should be tested whenever possible so that mistakes can be spotted. An element of 'control' should always be included, this is normally asking for the same information in a different way, to check the validity and consistency of the respondent.

There are a number of simple rules to follow:

- Use yes/no or multiple choice questions whenever possible and treat open-ended answers with caution

- Avoid asking for people's opinions, ask for facts

- Eliminate ambiguity

- Make sure that the respondent understands the question

- Manner and appearance of interviewer might influence answers

- The respondent may answer certain questions in order to give a false idea of status or try to please

- Questions on the future provide misleading answers

- People's real attitudes are difficult to ascertain

- Respondents do not always know the reasons for their answers

- Respondent may not be the decision maker and the answers will not reflect the views of the decision maker

SAMPLING

In most cases it is impossible (or unnecessarily expensive) to research the entire target population and a sample will have to be used. There are some very complex statistical rules for sampling and these will be followed if an agency project is undertaken − these are called probability or random samples. For the type of research undertaken in-house by smaller businesses it is unlikely that purely random samples will be a practical proposition.

It is much more likely that a sample will be selected according to knowledge of the market and with reference to the information required. The basic principle to be followed is that the sample must be as representative as possible. If you are questioning customers, make sure that all sizes are considered, different types are represented and that regional bias is eliminated. Make allowances for as many variables as possible − age, sex, occupation, location, disposable incomes, nature of business, etc.

USING THE INFORMATION

It is worth stressing that, no matter how much research you do, and how sophisticated it is, if it is not analysed in a meaningful way and not applied correctly to the decision making process, there is not much point in doing it in the first place. The object of marketing research is not to reinforce the pre-conceived ideas of the business owner or

THE BRITISH MOTORIST AND HIS CAR

YOUR CURRENT CAR

*PLEASE COMPLETE THE QUESTIONNAIRE BY
MARKING YOUR ANSWER IN THE APPROPRIATE BOX THUS* ✓

(1-3)	(4)	(5)	(6-9)	(10)
	5			5

Firstly, we would like some information about the car which you currently own, that is the car of which you are the principal driver. Please fill in the details for the car named below.

1   What is the make (e.g. Ford, Talbot) and model (e.g. Escort, Sunbeam) of your current car?

   PLEASE WRITE IN: **Make:** _____   **Model:** _____   *(20-23)*

2   Which of the following apply to your current car?
   PLEASE TICK ONE BOX IN EACH COLUMN

Automatic gear change	☐₁	Petrol	☐₁	2 doors	☐₁
Manual gear change without overdrive	☐₂	Diesel	☐₂	2 doors plus rear door	☐₂
Manual gear change with overdrive/5th forward gear	☐₃ *(26)*	Other fuel	☐₃ *(27)*	4 doors	☐₃
				4 doors plus rear door	☐₄
				Estate car/Station wagon	☐₅ *(28)*

3a   Which of the following comes closest to describing the paint colour of your car?

Black	☐₁	Yellow	☐₁	Brown	☐₁
White/cream	☐₂	Green	☐₂	Orange	☐₂
Beige	☐₃	Blue	☐₃	Purple	☐₃ *(31)*
Grey	☐₄ *(29)*	Red	☐₄ *(30)*		

3b   Would you say it is a light shade or a dark shade of this colour?

   A light shade ☐₁   A dark shade ☐₂ *(32)*

3c   Is it a metallic or standard finish?

   Metallic ☐₁   Standard ☐₂ *(33)*

AND NOW COULD YOU ANSWER SOME QUESTIONS ABOUT YOURSELF
THIS INFORMATION WILL BE USED FOR STATISTICAL PURPOSES ONLY.

A. Age:

	under 25 ☐ $_1$	35 – 44 ☐ $_3$	55 – 64 ☐ $_5$
	25 – 34 ☐ $_2$	45 – 54 ☐ $_4$	65+ ☐ $_6$ *(65)*

B. Sex:

Male ☐ $_1$ Female ☐ $_2$ *(66)*

C. Marital status

Single ☐ $_1$ Married ☐ $_2$ *(67)*

D. How many adults (including yourself) are there over 15 years of age living in your household?

One ☐ $_1$ Two ☐ $_2$ Three ☐ $_3$ Four or more ☐ $_4$ *(68)*

And how many children aged between 6 and 14 years?

None ☐ $_0$ One ☐ $_1$ Two ☐ $_2$ Three ☐ $_3$ Four or more ☐ $_4$ *(69)*

And how many infants under 6?

None ☐ $_0$ One ☐ $_1$ Two ☐ $_2$ Three ☐ $_3$ Four or more ☐ $_4$ *(70)*

E. Are you the chief wage earner in your household?

Yes ☐ $_1$ No ☐ $_2$ *(71)*

F. Are you in full or part-time employment?

I am in full-time employment ☐ $_1$

I am in part-time employment ☐ $_2$

I am not in paid employment ☐ $_3$ *(72)*

G. Which of the following best describes your occupation?

Unskilled worker ☐ $_1$		Senior Management ☐ $_1$
Skilled worker ☐ $_2$		Professional ☐ $_2$
Farming, Fishing, Forestry, etc. ☐ $_3$		Self employed ☐ $_3$
Secretarial/Clerical ☐ $_4$		Housewife/student/retired ☐ $_4$ *(74)*
Middle Management ☐ $_5$ *(73)*		

H. Which of the following best describes the level at which you completed your formal education or training?

Primary/Secondary School without qualifications ☐ $_1$	Higher education – not university ☐ $_4$
Primary/Secondary School with qualifications ☐ $_2$	University ☐ $_5$ *(75)*
Professional/Technical training ☐ $_3$	

PLEASE RETURN THIS QUESTIONNAIRE IN THE STAMPED
ENVELOPE PROVIDED WITHIN TEN DAYS.

Research Services Ltd.,Station House, Harrow Road, Wembley, Middlesex, England.

J2654 (77-80)

manager or to feed his ego. The reason for objective marketing research, secondary and primary, is to reduce the risks and facilitate better decision making.

Effective marketing research will not eliminate risk and does not remove the need for initiative and entrepreneurial skill. It will help the business owner or manager to set up and develop a better business and make better business decisions. But it still takes care and intelligence to apply the results of research to well identified problems.

PRIMARY RESEARCH

CHECKLIST

1 Have you considered using primary marketing research to help provide better terms of reference for your business decisions?

2 Do you understand the range of questions that marketing research may help to answer?

3 If you use research to provide better marketing information do you *always* go to secondary sources first?

4 Have you considered the advantages of using a marketing research agency to provide information on a major decision?

5 If you decide you have a marketing problem that can be helped by using research do you plan a logical approach to the project?

6 Are you aware of the advantages and disadvantages of the various methods of primary marketing research?

7 Do you understand the criteria for constructing an objective and successful questionnaire?

8 Do you consider all variables when constructing a sample?

9 When provided with a well researched report do you use it, even if you don't agree with its conclusions?

PART III
Sales
&
Distribution

FACTORY OUTPUT

SALES FORCE

THE DEAL IS MADE

PRODUCTS DELIVERED

WHOLESALER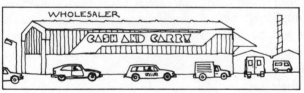

RETAILER

CUSTOMER

5
Selling

Many small firms employ salesmen but even more must rely on the owner or other managers to perform the task of direct selling. This will depend on the size of the firm and on the product or service it is providing. A company producing specialist computer software is unlikely to require a large independent salesforce, although it would be difficult to envisage a successful local newspaper without any advertisement sales staff. Whatever the case, except in very rare circumstances, somebody will have to sell.

The sales process, which is common to all sales activity, is a basic routine comprising six steps all of which will have to be accomplished before a sale is made. Some or all of these steps will be undertaken by whoever does the direct selling although some may be achieved by advertising or sales promotion. Initial contact has to be made with prospects and their interest aroused in the product or service on offer. It is vital, especially in industrial selling, to ensure that the person approached is one who can actually make a decision about buying. No customer ever has a limitless supply of funds; there are always choices, either between suppliers of the same product or service or, where the purchase is a non-essential, between different (sometimes completely different) products and services or, of course, buying nothing at all. Therefore, a preference must be created for the goods or services on offer.

During the sales process one or more <u>specific proposals</u> must be made to the customer, and this will be followed at some stage by a move which <u>closes the sale</u>. Although there are many different methods employed by salesmen during the lead-up to and the discussion itself, there must always be a moment reached when the sale is closed; all of the activities undertaken previously will be directed towards this goal.

But the selling job does not end here. <u>Retaining business</u> is the final, and often most important part, of the sales process. Clearly, the customer must be satisfied with the purchase and this means <u>not</u> making unjustified claims for the product or service. The purchase must be delivered on time, in the right condition and, finally, the whole transaction must be backed by adequate after-sales service. Ensuring all this happens is almost always the direct responsibility of the salesman as he or she is the person in contact with the customer.

No salesman should ever attempt to sell without the support of relevant presentation material. Quite often this will be in the form of documentation and printed promotional material, although there is wide use of audio-visual, samples and demonstration. It is essential that all material is professionally produced, is relevant to the sale in hand, and is understood fully by the salesman. Blithe chatter alone is not enough and in many cases can actually have a negative result. Most buyers appreciate good, accurate and well presented facts; they are usually busy people and salesmen must remember that the buyer <u>always</u> has a choice.

PEOPLE THAT SELL

Some businesses start up with great plans; they offer a good product or service, back it with some reasonable promotion, and then the owners sit back and wait for the customers to come flocking in — these businesses don't usually last very long. On the other hand there are people who go out and look for customers but when they find prospects they discuss the weather, the local football team or the latest rates demand, and they as they are leaving turn round and say: 'By the way, here's my card. We deal in office cleaning (or printing/delivery/double-glazing, etc). If you need any help please give me a call.' The customers never do call and the business fails.

With the exception of mail order, in *every* business somebody has to actively *sell*. Even if it is only to tie up one or two contracts a year, a business with no salesman is no business.

In the early stages many small firms depend on the principal or other senior managers for personal selling, taking on extra sales staff as business grows. Others need a sales team from the start. Whatever the case, employment legislation, salaries, overheads, operating expenses and the fickle nature of people make the employment of sales staff a major, and risky, undertaking.

Do I need sales staff?

The overriding factor when considering the employment of sales staff is money; whether individuals will bring in enough profits to cover their costs, and whether the company has the resources to carry them whilst they are training or if they go through a bad patch. The small business owner or manager must always remember that there are options: concentrating efforts on indirect selling and backing these up with limited direct action by themselves; marketing by mail order; or leaving the selling to agents. These options are fully examined elsewhere in this book.

It is expensive to have a salesman make a personal visit to a prospective customer. Even if the salesman is working efficiently the cost to the firm is unlikely to be less than £15 to £20 a visit.

The *value of the product* or *average order size* is therefore an important factor. The cost of an insurance policy or desk-top computer provides sufficient margin from a sale to allow adequate return on sales effort, taking into account all the unproductive calls. Similarly, if a salesman is visiting wholsesalers with, say, cuddly toys, the order size should bring in enough to cover the cost of his visit. This would not be the case if the cuddly toy salesman sold direct to end-customers or even to retailers. In a trade where there is a lot of repeat business salesmen will be out looking for new customers and a sales office will deal with future orders. Here, a sale coming from the original visit may not be cost effective in itself, but the firm will rely on the repeat business to repay its sales effort.

The *numbers and distribution of customers* are important factors when considering whether or not to employ sales staff, and how many people should be in the team. Many small firms operate on a local basis and the concentrated nature of the target market often makes it worthwhile considering a sales team. This is especially true when the product or service is used by a wide range of customers – office equipment, printing services and home improvements are good examples. A specialist plastic moulder is not likely to find it very rewarding to operate a large sales force and so will rely on generating enquiries and concentrating its sales effort on those.

All these factors, together with the broad objectives of the business, high price market skimming for example, and the availability of alternative methods of distribution will influence the final decisions. Do we need a sales force? If so how large should it be and how will it be organised?

But sales people are notoriously difficult to handle; in a small business they will require a great deal of self-motivation and must be able to manage themselves and their activities. Beware the shallow extrovert, the person that lays on the charm with no real sincerity. Salesmen in small firms have to organise themselves, work hard and bring in the business. A low achiever (and it can take months to spot one) can spell disaster.

TRAINING

Selling involves a number of skills which must first be learnt and then further developed over a period of time. The role of training is vital (and often overlooked) for the smaller company requiring maximum return from its limited resources; it must be considered an important investment, not an extravagance.

Sales training is required in the following areas:
● Selling technique
● Management technique
● Product understanding
● The market

Time must be allowed for new sales staff to get to know the product or service, the market — customers and competitors and how the company operates. A conscious effort must be made to teach salesmen this basic information. It is neither reasonable nor productive to set new sales staff to work without adequate in-firm training.

Business owners and managers will be well rewarded if they also provide facilities for the development of technique — selling and management. If the company is large enough to have an experienced sales manager (or if one of the directors has a background in sales) then training may be performed in-company, but it must have a formal basis and it is essential to provide the right atmosphere — away from telephones and other disturbances. Regular training sessions linked with sales meetings provide an effective technique practiced by many businesses, large and small.

For the very small business there are a number of excellent

short courses run by reliable organisations. Sales staff should
be sent on an initial course if they are new to selling and then
allowed to attend development courses on a regular basis.
Trade associations sometimes offer courses in selling and
details of commercially available schemes may be found in
the marketing press.

BUYER BEHAVIOUR

Economists base their theories on a number of assumptions,
one of which is that people behave in an economically
rational way. The theory is that every buying decision is
determined only by financial considerations; having examined
all opportunities in the market the buyer makes his or her
choice and takes the cheapest option. Economic man always
acts rationally to further his own financial well-being.

This theory, whilst having its uses to economists, just
doesn't hold if applied to real life marketing. If it did, there
would only be one type of car, one place where everyone
went on holiday, one type of clothing and only one business
– the State. We all behave in an irrational way and nowhere
is it more evident than in our buying behaviour.

It is generally true that industrial buyers act more rationally
than consumers, indeed most study of buying behaviour has
been focussed upon end-consumers. But industrial buyers are
only human and subject to their own weaknesses and preju-
dices, and to outside influences.

A basic understanding (or at least recognition) of buying
behaviour, and the factors that influence it, is especially
useful to anyone involved in marketing products and services.
In the context of this book it can most easily be applied to
direct selling activity. But it must be remembered that
knowledge of what motivates and influences buying decisions
is equally important to all marketing activities.

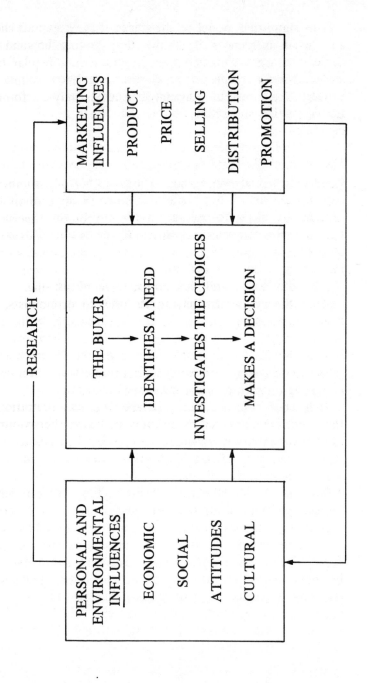

Fig. 5.1. The buying decision and how it is influenced

This simplified model of the stages of the buying decision, and what influences it, shows that buying behaviour is subject to a great many non-economic pressures. Marketing alone creates a complex of pressures, not only on the decision process itself but on shaping attitudes; in the short-term through persuasive selling, and in the long-term with strategic campaigns.

Economic considerations must not be ignored, consumers have limited disposable incomes and businesses have budgets. Price is nearly always a major factor, as is value for money. And if a product is not available because of poor distribution it is hardly likely to sell very well. But to get a picture of how the salesman can best respond to the irrational behaviour of buyers we should look at the personal and environmental influences on decision making.

All individuals, and businesses, have needs. Apart from basic needs like notepaper, hunger and thirst, people have a need for pleasure, they seek security, self-esteem, and have an innate desire to own things. Salesmen should remember that their customers determine needs on different bases; salesmen can stimulate interest in products and services by appealing to the most appropriate need.

Behaviour is also affected by people's own attitudes, and their cultural and social influences. Many purchases are rooted in status or self-image — the size and quality of an office desk, the coffee-table book or the smart car. Others are affected by family pressure, or by ethnic and religious influences — labour-saving devices, food and toiletries. Fashion plays an all too familiar role.

Although it is impossible to go into the details of all these complex behavioural influences in this book, the knowledge of their existence is useful to the salesman — business owner or member of a sales team. Recognising the way a particular prospect is behaving and how best a need can be generated are extremely valuable tools for the direct sales situation, to say nothing about the way a business approaches its entire marketing effort.

THE SALES PROCESS

Planning

Before entering the nitty-gritty of approaching prospects and making sales, there is a lot of work to be done. Much of a salesman's time is taken up with planning. Not the type of planning covered in the next chapter – territories, time, goals and targets; but simply establishing the best prospects and finding out the right contacts within those prospects. For some it is a case of going through the 'Yellow Pages' or other local directories, others will determine prime neigh-bourhoods and work through them, and for the specialists it is a case of trade publications and directories.

After this initial research has provided a list the next step is to narrow it down; the most attractive prospects may be selected by applying suitable criteria. Do we deal with very small businesses? Are these properties likely to require renovation? Will this firm generate a lot of print? Does this type of retailer have a security problem?

Once a list of likely prospects has been established the salesman must determine exactly who to contact – who makes the buying decision. It is a complete waste of time making an elaborate pitch to a housewife in the afternoon, if it is her husband who will make the decision. This is nearly always the case for major purchases – home exten-sions, insurance policies and durables. If you deal in office supplies, company buyers will usually be the best people to approach, but they will not have the authority to pur-chase machinery – that will be the responsibility of the works or production manager, or managing director in smaller firms.

Finding out who makes the decision in particular cases

is a difficult task. Experience will help a lot and the salesman will get to recognise the signs. A preliminary telephone call to the managing director's secretary, or a chat to the receptionist, may reveal all, but often the salesman will have to find out on the first visit, and fast. Once a manager has indicated that he is in a position to make a decision it is virtually impossible to get him to admit later that he cannot. The general rule is to start at the top and, if need be, work down until you reach the right person. This has the added benefit of being able to say to a decision-making manager: 'I've been talking to your managing director and he says . . .'

Initial contact

Enquiries may be generated through advertising, leaflets, mail shots or at exhibitions and fairs. If so, initial contact has been made, and because the enquirer has already shown an interest, the salesman is off to a flying start. But there are not many businesses where sufficient enquiries can be generated through promotion. The failure rate between initial contact and successful sale is inevitably high with losses at every stage of the sales process (see fig. 5.2 opposite) − plenty of prospects need to be established and contact made.

Salesmen will need to canvas for prospects. While 'cold calling' (visiting prospects with no appointment), suits certain businesses, as the main method of canvassing it is generally to be avoided. It is wasteful in terms of time and resources although can often be used on an opportunist basis during planned sales activity. Much better is to use the telephone to arrange a meeting, or better still send a letter and follow it up with a telephone call to make an appointment.

Fig. 5.2. The sales process

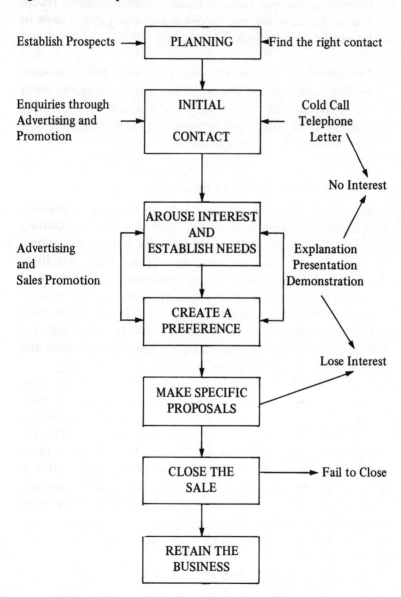

A general point on technique which applies here and at all stages in the sales process. Ask questions that demand positive answers. For example: 'Would Wednesday or Friday be best for me to come and see you?' *not* 'May I come and see you sometime?'

Use questions to lead the prospect on to the next point getting approval on the point just made; regularly recap on decisions already made with questions that demand agreement or direct the prospect towards making a positive decision. Never let the prospect say no.

Arouse interest and establish needs

This part of the process may well be commenced on the telephone and continued at the first meeting. Asking the prospect if he has used a similar service or bought a similar product before, the salesman should establish what was liked and disliked about it. The salesman should then show how his product or service is better on each point.

Next a need should be established. If the acquisition will save money, or make it, show how. If it will enhance status, illustrate it with an example. Once interest is aroused and a need established the prospect is on the salesman's side and ready to listen to more.

Create a preference

All products and services have advantages over competitors, real or constructed; create unique selling points (USPs) with which to sell yours. It might offer a wider range of sizes or colours, it may have certain features not found on competitors' models, your company offers better service, quicker delivery, easy terms or will meet the client's specifications.

The salesman must explain the benefits of dealing with

his company and back up any claims with evidence — samples, letters from satisfied customers, press cuttings and reference material. The case must be supported with effective visual presentation (see later) and a demonstration offered if appropriate. But the visual material and demonstration must not come too early in the pitch. Aids must be used to support a case, not compete by offering distraction or by making unrelated points, however valid. One point must be made at a time moving steadily along a planned route closing on a positive note at each stage.

If the product or service is a complex one or needs to be 'made to measure' then the salesman must not rush. The first meeting can be used to gather information, establish needs and determine terms of reference. Another appointment will then be made and the salesman should go away and prepare a sound case based on facts known to be true. The sales presentation will then be made at the second or subsequent meeting.

Make specific proposals

If the salesman has reached this far he must not back away. Specific proposals must be made at this stage. 'When shall we deliver, next week or the week after?' 'Do you want the leather topped desk or the veneer?' 'If you order today I can arrange a 5% discount.' 'Will you pay cash or would you like me to arrange credit?'

The salesman will meet with objections which must be overcome systematically. Some will arise because the prospect simply has not understood a point about the product or what the salesman has said. Others will not be so easy to deal with, they may be based on legitimate weaknesses in what is on offer. When these objections arise the subject must be changed and the salesman should shift the prospect's attention to benefits that have already been agreed. If that doesn't work the salesman must admit the weakness but measure it against a list of all the advantages on offer. If the disadvantages genuinely outweigh the benefits there is little chance of closing the sale, and if the prospect is conned, there is every chance of losing a lot of good will and any opportunity for business later.

Close the sale

This is where the salesman gets the final commitment; the prospect becomes a customer. The salesman must be in a position to allow the prospect to sign an order there and then. Time must not be given for reconsideration. The salesman cannot leave himself in a position of having to come back later with an order form; or even worse, send it through the post. Once the signature is on the order the customer has to be made to feel good. All the agreed benefits should be reinforced and the customer reassured that the right decision has been made.

Retain the business

But things have not ended because the salesman has got a customer's signature on an order form. The salesman is responsible for ensuring that the goods are delivered on time and in good order, or that the service he has sold is carried out satisfactorily. If his company depends on repeat orders the salesman should make regular visits to ensure everything is going smoothly. Customers should not be overstocked (often done under the guise of a special offer or quantity discount), this always leads to discontent by the customer and risks a lot of future business. **Good will is the stock in trade of the effective salesman.**

After-sales service is a marketing responsibility and consumer legislation has made it difficult for any company to shirk its duty. As the main, often only, contact between the selling company and the customer, the salesman is normally the person to whom complaints are directed. He must therefore be prepared to deal with them. Too many salesmen are interested only in getting orders, failing to realise that adequate after-sales care is in their own best long-term interests.

PRESENTATION MATERIAL

There are few sales presentations that do not benefit from good visual back-up. The most commonly used, apart from samples of the product itself, is printed material. There is, however, increasing use of other techniques such as slide projection, charts and cassette messages. All these have their roles and are used to great effect by many salesmen working for large and small businesses. The aid must be compatible with the type of product or service it is portraying: technical diagrams work well on charts; holidays, photographic services and property deals lend themselves to slides; and hard-hitting messages can be professionally presented on a cassette.

But almost every salesman will use a number of printed aids in the course of his presentation. Price list, brochures, testimonials, specification sheets and explanatory leaflets are all used from time to time and it is most important to present this material in an attractive and professional way. The most usual, and certainly the best way, is to use a plastic folder – the type that contains a number of clear pockets. Every salesman has his own method of making a presentation so it is vital that each makes up his own folder with his own selection of material. As the salesman makes the presentation he will use a particular part of the folder to support a point he is making. He must be careful not to confuse by using a visual support which makes a different point to the one being made verbally. The prospect must not be given the folder and allowed to look through it – it will not sell, the salesman must do that.

Effective presentation using clear, precise and honest

language supported with meaningful visual material will make sales and leave the door open for future business. Sharp practice and unsupportable claims backed with banal drivel should be left to the cowboys.

SELLING

CHECKLIST

1. Have you identified who in your business is actively doing the selling?

2. Should you employ a sales force?
   i) Is the unit price or average order size large enough to allow a return on personal sales visits?
   ii) Does the number and distribution of your potential customers make it a sensible proposition to employ a sales team?
   iii) Is it normal practice in your trade for salesmen to make personal visits or should you use another method of marketing?

3. If you or your senior colleagues do the selling, have you made any effort to undertake sales training? If you employ sales staff do they get initial and development training in product, market and technique?

4. Have you considered why people buy your particular product or service? Are there any other factors affecting the buying decision that you could utilise to bring influence on prospective buyers of your product or service?

5. Do you and/or your salesmen make every effort to reach the decision makers in all the best prospects?

6. Have you studied the sales process and ensured that your sales effort is structured around it?

7. Do sales presentations made to your prospects include the use of the most suitable visual aid?

8. Do you and/or your salesmen prepare and use a professional-looking folder of support printed material?

6
Sales Management

Selling is 90% about organisation: organisation which comes from self-discipline and a well managed marketing environment. Whether sales are achieved by a national sales force or individually by the owners or managers, the role of effective sales management is paramount in obtaining success.

Identification is the first priority; identification of the prospects, and identification of the decision makers. A supplier of office materials will have an almost limitless range of prospects but effective management will identify those that offer the optimum return. A manufacturer of a range of specialist machine tools will have a very limited market and here, management should ensure maximum exploitation of that limited market.

As with all marketing activity, planning is of major importance to the sales and distribution function. Budgets and targets must be set, with profits as the major objective, but always within the realms of the possible. Nothing is more demoralising for a salesman than never to achieve targets; and nothing is less useful to a company than reaching targetted sales – only to find that it has in fact made a thumping great loss.

Time is a crucial factor. Many studies have shown that salesmen spend more time on non-productive activities such as travelling, waiting and reporting than they spend on selling. Good organisation of territories, routes,

transport and customer contact-time maximises selling
effort and is the responsibility of whoever does the selling.
A sales force will also need firm guidance and support from
a sympathetic manager.

Salesmen must feel part of a team, they must know as
much as possible about their jobs and what they are selling,
and they must understand their role as profit earners. Salesmen should have access to financial information which will
allow them to make the best deals, in the interest of the
company. Motivation comes from effective planning, good
day to day man management and thorough training. Even the
best salesmen require regular training in product knowledge
and technique. A good sales force is one that is fully involved
in the affairs of the company.

Reporting is the most disliked part of any salesman's
work. Salesmen develop a flair for dealing with people but
are notoriously badly organised and take to paperwork like
fish to flying. On the other hand, good management can
only be effected if managers have sufficient information —
the sales manager will have to reconcile these conflicting
interests. Sales are the life blood of any business and the
best results come from a combination of good sales practice backed by effective sales management.

PLANNING

Having established exactly what role personal selling will
play in the marketing mix, the business owner or manager
is faced with the problem of managing that activity. If he
or she is to perform the sales function there is no less requirement for effective planning and forecasting. But, if a sales
team is employed, the entire management function becomes
so crucial to the success of the business that it becomes,
arguably, the most important job of the lot.

Management starts with planning, both in terms of the
wider implications for the company's performance, and in

terms of the day-to-day operation of the personal selling activity. We can say that planning goes through four stages, each of which should be taken in turn by the sales manager. (NOTE: For the purposes of this chapter the expression sales manager refers to the person managing the personal selling function rather than any formal title. It may be the owner or manager of the business or an executive managing a sales force).

Four stages of planning

Objectives that are specific to sales activity must be set; they must be measurable in finite terms. Forecasting will provide a guide to the sales manager as an indication of a reasonable target for the business as a whole. This can be further divided to give targets (or budgets) for individual sales staff. Objectives must fit in with the overall company plan and considered in terms of achievable levels of sales and profits, and of the costs involved in reaching the sales targets.

Resources must be determined in relation to the objectives set. The sales manager will have certain resources at his disposal: staff, dealers and distributors, and will know what back-up is planned in the firm's other promotional activities. The manager then has to allocate these resources in a way that will best meet the set objectives, or determine what further resources will be necessary. If additional resources are needed but not likely to be made available, the objectives will have to be revised.

Methods through which sales objectives may be achieved must be implemented with care and consideration. The manager must decide in which way the job is to be tackled. But it is not good enough just to do the obvious — a range of methods should be considered and a creative approach taken to devise as many alternatives to the obvious as possible. For example, emphasis may be placed on cold calling – sending salesmen out in their cars to call on as many people as possible – alternatively they may use the telephone to make appointments or even to sell. But it may be better to run a series of seminars to which the most likely prospects are invited.

Operational planning, first and foremost, puts the set objectives into the context of time, with reference to the available resources and the methods to be employed. Sales objectives become targets when placed within the limitations of time, and budgets when contingent costs are considered. The sales manager must create schedules for each activity and estimate the costs that will be involved. The other part of operational planning comes with setting up machinery for the control of sales activity, and to allow for adequate reporting-back facilities – in other words, paperwork. Without records that work no management operation can run smoothly, if at all. Nobody really likes paperwork so the secret is to keep it simple, useful and to a minimum.

FORECASTING AND TARGETS

Sales forecasting simply involves taking a systematic approach to estimating future sales. There is no golden rule, almost every manager takes a different approach to the task; large companies actually employ economists especially for the job. The informed guess is the most usual method employed in the smaller business and even this is prefereable to the other common practice of adding an arbitrary across-the-board percentage increase to the previous year's sales.

There are, however, some simple guidelines that may be adopted to provide better quality forecasts without involving great expense in time and money. When reasonable targets are required, the more accurate the forecasts on which the figures are based, the better, and sales managers will benefit from the application of a little science.

Forecasts can be made for the short-term – up to one year; the medium-term – three to five years; and long-term – anything up to 25 years. The value of long-term forecasts is questionable (a fact readily agreed by the Chancellor of the Exchequer) and, in any case, totally impractical for the smaller business. Even medium-term forecasts are rarely of any practical value to the smaller business which is so susceptible to outside influences and prone to radical changes such as rapid growth.

We start our process of forecasting from the company's own records; how it has performed in the recent past. Taking the previous year's figures month by month a graph may be constructed as follows:

Sales:

Jan	Feb	Mar	Apr	May	Jun	Jul	Aug	Sep	Oct	Nov	Dec
100	80	60	140	60	130	120	130	70	120	110	90

Fig. 6.1. Monthly Sales

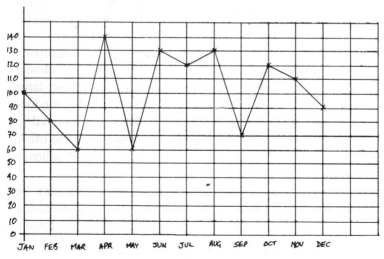

But this graph shows a somewhat erratic picture and it is difficult to determine the trends and seasonal fluctuation and impossible to guess where the curve is going next. To get any real picture we must smooth the curve so that it tells us the overall pattern; we do this by producing a *moving average*. We simply take the figures for a period, say 3 months, average them and use that figure on the graph in place of the actual figure. Moving along one month at a time the same sum is repeated until the end of the year is reached.

For example:	December (previous year)		=	60	+
	January		=	100	+
	February		=	80	+
		Total		240	
	Divide by three:	Average	=	80	

Next figure:	January		=	100	+
	February		=	80	+
	March		=	60	+
		Total		240	
	Divide by three:	Average	=	80	

July figure:	June		=	130	+
	July		=	120	+
	August		=	130	+
		Total		380	
	Divide by three:	Average	=	127	

Figures for the year and the moving average graph, compared with the erratic version, are as follows.

	(Dec)	Jan	Feb	Mar	Apr	May	Jun	Jul	Aug	Sep	Oct	Nov	Dec
Sales	60	100	80	60	140	60	130	120	130	70	120	110	90
3-monthly total		240	240	280	260	330	310	380	320	320	300	320	
Average		80	80	93	87	110	103	127	107	107	100	107	

Fig. 6.2. **Three-monthly moving average**

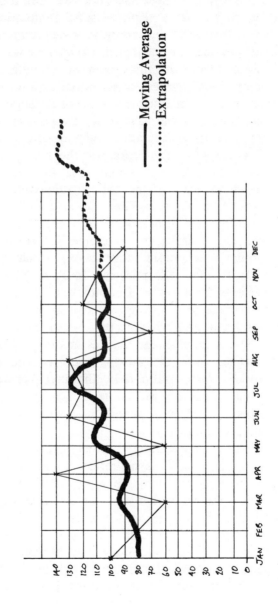

The moving average has smoothed out the company's sales figures so that a slight seasonal fluctuation can be clearly seen. But, more importantly, a steady increase in sales over the year can be identified; a fact that was not easily determinable from the first graph. A reference to graphs of previous years' figures (which usually show a similar pattern) will prove that last year was not exceptional. If it was, the sales manager will have to try to discover why and take the reasons into consideration when making his forecast.

A graphical prediction of the next year's sales can be made by simply extending the moving average curve as shown in Fig 6.2 and this extrapolation can be used as a basis for forecasting. There are arithmetic methods of extrapolation, and other ways to make predictions (regression analysis, correlation, econometric models, etc.) but all require much more information, which is difficult to find and often of little relevance to a smaller company; demand patterns for example. For most smaller businesses a graphical projection of a moving average curve is the easiest and the best method on which to base sales forecasts.

The sales manager may estimate monthly sales forecasts working from the moving average. The fact that targets will be less erratic than the previous years' actual performances is no bad thing – a more regular sales pattern helps the business operation, especially with stockholding and production.

But before coming to final forecasts, the sales manager must take into consideration a number of other factors.

These factors may be represented as shown in Fig 6.3 which indicates that the factors become narrower in influence as they get closer to the business itself. Influences move from the general – the state of the economy, to the very specific – the individual performance of individual salesmen. Examples of the type of factors that may influence the final forecasts are as follows:

The economy Is the recession getting worse?
            Are your customers getting EEC grants?
            Are they paying less tax?

Your industry Are you operating in a dying trade?
               Is there a major new competitor?
               What is the import tariff situation?

The company Has it changed its marketing objectives?
             Are there any major promotions coming up?
             Have you got a new managing director?

Products   What stage in the life-cycle?
                Any new products or new packaging?
                Have there been changes in fashion?

Sales Team   Is it the same size?
                Have you just lost your best salesman?
                Is there a new incentive scheme?

An informed view of the effect of these influences, and any
others that are evident, will indicate an optimistic or pessi-
mistic view of the overall figures and indicate special considerations for certain parts of the year. The final forecasts,
annual and monthly, should be treated accordingly.

Targets

If there is just one salesman the forecast is the target. If
there is a team, the sales manager has the task of setting
targets for each member of the team. *This does not mean
dividing the sales forecast figure by the number of salesmen and giving each that figure as his or her target.*

The sales manager will know who in his team are the
best performers, the potential of each territory, past history
of each territory and other circumstances surrounding each
individual in the sales team. Working within the framework
of the overall forecast, targets must be created for each
salesman on an annual, monthly and even weekly basis.
As the year progresses a better and better idea of how each
salesman is performing will be obtained from regular sales
analyses prepared by the manager (see later). These analyses
must include a 'year to date' figure for both target and
achieved sales – this is the best all-round indication of how
things are going because, as we have seen above, the fluctuations have been taken out of the targets through the moving
analysis forecast. It is worth noting that a moving average

analysis may be used for each territory to aid setting individual targets.

Targets must be attainable, and *recognised* as such by the salesmen. The key task for every member of the sales team, including the manager, is to reach target sales. If targets are unreasonable, (a practice sometimes used in the mistaken belief it will motivate salesmen) the only result will be demoralisation and eventual alienation of the sales team. If there is a range of products or services, targets should be set for each item or group of items.

THE SALES ORGANISATION

For many small businesses the employment of a field sales team or inside sales staff (the principles are just the same for retailers) is an inevitable consequence of being in business. Others may just decide that using a direct sales force is the best way to market their product or service. Whatever the case, it is a huge expense and a great commitment, and consequently must be tuned to the finest degree — and that means the best possible management and organisation.

The sales manager

Being a sales manager is a full-time job (reading this chapter should convince any doubter) and one should be employed as soon as is practicable. Even if there are only two or three salesmen, one must be made the manager, in function if not in title, and given time to manage. But with a larger team, the practice of giving a territory (or responsibility for national accounts) to a sales manager is to be avoided. The employment of a full-time manager, providing he is competent, will more than reward a business by increased sales and greater efficiency.

The function of sales management is wide, involving both paperwork and fieldwork. There is a growing tendency, a

very good one, for sales managers to spend most of their
time in the field working with, and encouraging their staff,
leaving the paperwork for the evenings and weekends – they
are generally well rewarded for this effort and commitment.

A sales manager's first task is forecasting, a job normally
done in conjunction with other senior managers, and setting
sales targets. He or she must recruit and select sales staff,
budget, control, train, lead and motivate the sales team and
ensure there is adequate administration to deal with enquiries
and orders. But sales managers also have the responsibility
to liaise with other departments in order to ensure continuity
of effort. And at the end of the day, it is the sales manager
who is responsible for meeting the company's sales objectives.

Recruitment and selection

On average, staff turnover in sales is between 15% and 20%
a year, any more or less usually indicates a problem, and this
means that recruiting and selecting new people is a continuous
process. Before looking for candidates, a clear picture of
what is required must be firmly fixed: qualifications, job
description, remuneration – salary and other, and likely
career pattern. A constant watch must be kept for likely
prospects but it is most likely that advertising will be necessary to attract better candidates. Advertisements should
contain details of all the above points as well as product
and company information, it is not worth skimping on
the ads.

Applicants should complete a comprehensive application form and references *must* be taken up – preferably
by telephone. Initial interviews narrow down the field and
a pre-prepared checklist, itemising the qualities required
and how the candidate fits the bill, is carefully completed.
Having organised all the relevant information, a final interview and selection are made. Headhunting is a useful way
of finding suitable applicants but the formal selection procedure should *never* be omitted.

CONTROL AND MOTIVATION

Sales managers must play the numbers game. They should know, for their business, how many initial contacts must be made to generate one enquiry; how many enquiries must be followed up to get one face-to-face interview; and how many face-to-face interviews must be made to close a sale. Armed with these figures together with the size of an average order and the targets, the manager is in a position to monitor his sales team.

Salesmen must maintain up-to-date contact cards for their territories and the manager must make sure they do. A boxed card-index is the best method; kept in alphabetical order they should contain details on every contact made.

- Company name, address, telephone number.
- Name of contact or contacts.
- Diary record of all activities: cold call, mail shot, letter, telephone call, interview and order details.
- Useful information: existing supplier, size of work-force, turnover, other business interests, etc.

Using the numbers information, the sales manager may use the contact records, which are presented regularly in analysis form (see Reporting), to discover if any particular salesman is not doing enough work or having unusual success. Finding the reasons behind the deviation from the norm quickly gives an indication of what the manager should do to keep the team in line.

Nobody really knows why but the 80/20 rule works for nearly every sales operation. It states that 80% of a firm's business comes from 20% of its customers — the 20% become the firm's major accounts. Ideally every salesman should have his or her fair share of them and these big accounts must receive special attention. Salesmen must be made fully aware of who their big accounts are and how important they are. A disproportionate amount of their, and their manager's time will be spent on developing existing big accounts and finding new ones.

Sales staff working in the field require a great deal of motivation. Some will come from themselves, or they shouldn't be doing the job, but motivation must also come from the manager. Most salesmen work from home, visiting the office only occasionally (they should never be given desks, they will only sit at them). Because of this, they must be made to feel part of a team − training, regular communication and the right mixture of leadership and friendship must come from the sales manager. The manager must work regularly with each member of the sales team, in the field, visiting customers with them and offering help and advice. Meetings and conferences as well as the odd social occasion are highlights in an often lonely working life.

Salesmen also respond to recognition for their achievements (not just their shortcomings), if they do well they should be told so by the very highest authority. Whilst it is the complete package outlined here that provides the best sales effort, most of all salesmen respond to incentive. They must have adequate remuneration and reward must come with effort. There are very few cases where a commission element is not desirable but, likewise, very few times when a reasonable basic salary should not form the basis of a remuneration package.

Finally, sales staff will need to be equipped: brief case, samples (sample case), order forms, presentation material and promotional aids. Sales managers must ensure that equipment is available and that their sales staff look after it. The state of equipment and rate at which it is used up, is often the fastest way of judging how much work a salesman is doing. Car, dress and general appearance are all tools of the salesman's trade and it is the manager's job to make sure all are in order.

TERRITORIES AND TIME

Establishing territories is no easy task. For most smaller businesses territories will be based on geographical areas, but it is just as valid to use product groups or customer allocation as a basis (or a combination of any of them). If a business is essentially a local one and offers a degree of specialism then a product/customer basis sometimes makes good sense.

Territories should be allocated so that the division of potential business is proportionate to the salesman's abilities and provides each member of the team with ample opportunities. Territories are sometimes difficult to alter, but should never be considered sacrosanct. The best time to change them is at the beginning of the trading year, coinciding with new budgets.

Having established territories, salesmen will require guidance on the best use of time, both in terms of method and in routeing. Method will be determined by the sales manager, with reference to the particular skills of the salesmen concerned, on how the team is organised, the type of products or services and the customers.

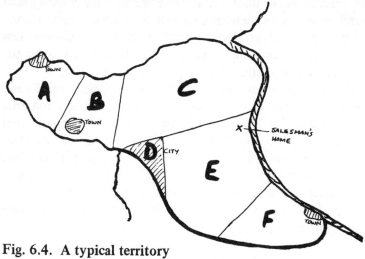

Fig. 6.4. A typical territory

Routeing, however, is simply a case of thorough planning and sensible control. The basic tools for this planning are a detailed map of the territory (preferably one containing business and industrial demography obtainable from a number of commercial sources), and a diary. In Fig 6.4 we have a diagram of an imaginary territory.

The territory has been sub-divided into six parts, the size of each part reflects its business potential. D is a city, A and B contain large towns, F a slightly smaller town and C and E are mostly rural. The salesman lives in the northeast corner of E and obviously would not be very smart if he visited customers in A and F on the same day.

Under the watchful eye and assistance of the sales manager, the salesman must focus attention on one particular zone at any one time. He must plan his time with great care using a call-sheet to write down, *in advance*, exactly which customers are to be visited, the name of the contact and the nature of the business. A large desk diary is an ideal document to use as a call-sheet. A number of activities may be carried out in the pre-determined zone on any one day, e.g. after-sales calls, interviews, demonstrations and cold calls, but planning the visits to minimise travelling time. Salesmen should travel to and from their territories *in their own time*.

Once the territory has been sub-divided the salesman will establish a routine by which he spends one day (or half-day) in a zone, doing business *only* in that zone on that day. This routine is entered into the diary at the beginning of each month (or, even better, year). No zone should be visited on the same day every week, zones should be rotated and the best way to ensure this is to have more or less than five zones, some allowance must be given for office visits and administration. Any enquiries or calls for assistance may be scheduled into the diary on the appropriate day.

REPORTING

Information is the life-blood of good management and, although they hate it, salesmen must be made to report regularly on their activities and to keep adequate records for themselves. The core of the salesman's own records will be his contact cards, up-dated each day, and his diary. This information should be transferred once a week on to a *Weekly Call Report* (see Fig 6.5) or on to a daily version if a lot of visits are involved.

Salesman . . . . Territory . . . . Week						
Non-call initial contacts this week Letter [ ] Telephone [ ]						
Day	Call	Inter-view	Order	Order size	Other	Remarks

Fig. 6.5. **Salesman's Weekly Call Report**

It should be strict policy that reports are sent to the manager, each week, on Friday evening. Information on order size should be checked against orders received (which should be sent in daily) and added to orders that have come in to the sales office direct from customers or other distributors. A form indicating weekly, monthly and year to date sales, target and achieved should be sent to each salesman by the following Tuesday. This immediate turn-round of sales information means that problems can be spotted and rapid response made by salesman and sales manager. A simple form adequate for this purpose is shown in Fig. 6.6.

Salesman . . . . Territory . . . . Week				
Period	Achieved	Target	Performance	Remarks
Week ending		1500		
Last month		4500		
Month to date		3000		
Year to date		19500		
(Sales Manager)				

Fig. 6.6. Weekly Sales Report

NOTE: This form, and all the other facsimile forms illustrated, shows only one set of figures. If the business deals with a range of products then figures will be required for each product or group of products.

Central to any effective sales operation is an efficient and competent sales office. This may only be one person, a secretary, but there *must* be someone in the office trained and able to deal with enquiries from customers, distributors and salesmen. Also, the sales office will need to process orders and ensure that they are correctly documented and dealt with by dispatch. Not having anybody with the information to deal with this administration is one of the quickest ways to destroy even the best sales efforts. The sales manager is responsible for this activity and for making sure that it runs smoothly.

Figure 6.7 shows a typical sales management form, the *Monthly Sales Analysis*. This provides the manager with information in a form that facilitates easy identification of problem areas and a reference with which he can monitor his entire sales activity. It shows, at a glance, the performance of each salesman and how things are going generally. A figure for centrally generated initial contacts (e.g. a national mail shot) can be added to provide a more accurate picture of response rates. As with other forms it may be arranged to show a number of products or product groups.

This information may be transferred on to a *Yearly Analysis* and totals, taken as a whole and divided salesman by salesman, will provide the data for the next year's marketing plan. Only by maintaining records regularly and systematically can effective management be carried out. These records will also help provide secondary research information for future projects. The new generation of micro-computers can provide the sales manager of today with a great deal of help, but however tedious keeping the records may be, they must be kept.

Activity	Salesman					TOTAL
Initial contacts						
Enquiries						
Contact/enquiry ratio						
Interview						
Enquiry/interview ratio						
Orders						
Indirect orders						
Interview/order ratio						
Value of orders						
Average order value						
Total sales						
Target sales						
Year to date total sales						
Year to date target sales						
Sales performance year to date						

Manager . . . . Region . . . . Month . . . .

Fig. 6.7. Monthly Sales Analysis

SALES MANAGEMENT

CHECKLIST

1 Have you set finite achievable sales objectives based on a scientific forecast?
2 Has each individual salesman been given weekly, monthly and annual sales targets?
3 Do you have resources necessary to meet objectives?
4 Do you regularly review the methods used for personal selling and constantly search for new creative ideas?
5 Have you a formal recruitment and selection procedure?
6 Have you produced a detailed salesman's job description?
7 Do you know: i) How many initial contacts needed for one enquiry?
      ii) How many enquiries for one interview/demonstration?
      iii) How many interviews/demonstrations for one order?
8 Do your salesmen maintain up-to-date contact cards?
9 Do you make a special effort to develop big accounts?
10 Does your sales manager spend enough time in the field?
11 Is there a commission element in your salesmen's pay?
12 Are your salesmen always well equipped?
13 Are your territories based on potential and abilities?
14 Do all your salesmen plan their work systematically using a call sheet/diary?
15 Do all your salesmen submit Weekly Call Reports *on time*?
16 Do you have a rapid response sales report-back system?
17 Do you have a sales office?
18 Does your sales manager maintain adequate sales records including sales activity ratios, and does he use them?

7
Distribution

Central to the whole of a firm's marketing strategy is the transfer of its goods and services to the final consumer. Often this transfer is made direct to the user: local services, mail order, commercial supplies, industrial components, etc., at other times distribution is achieved through one or more intermediaries: wholesalers, retailers, and industrial factors. Another option is to delegate marketing to agents or brokers who will sell the product or service leaving the company to physically transport the goods to the customers. The various methods of transfer are known as the <u>channels of distribution</u> and the selection of the best method or methods is a complex, often critical, and always fundamental decision for the smaller business.

Dealing directly with the final consumer has a number of advantages: the firm has direct control over all selling activities and can therefore plan more easily; profits aren't dissipated through intermediaries; the firm does not have to persuade another to merchandise its products; and it can more easily control the service provided to customers.

But it is not always possible for a smaller business to use direct means to distribute its goods or services even if logically that would be the best option. When there are many consumers spread over a large geographical area the resources

required to effectively reach the market are normally outside
the means of a small firm (often even a large one). Also many
intermediaries possess specialist skills in marketing which
cannot be matched by any manufacturer — indeed it would
be a tragic waste of resources if they tried.

Franchising is a method of distribution which, while
not new to Britain, has become increasingly popular over the
last few years. It accounts for a massive proportion of
retailing in this country as a way for firms to widen the
distribution of their goods and services. It also provides many
business opportunities for people who wish to work for
themselves or for existing businesses to expand their
operations.

Any businessman who has attempted to enter the field of
exporting will know that the path to success is riddled with
tripwires and a range of complexities that put off all but the
most determined and well informed. Finance, research,
documentation and transportation pose obvious problems,
but effective marketing is the key to success. Fortunately,
the businessman need not be alone in his misery; there is a
great deal of help at hand — assistance with finding agents,
market research, using language, and producing promotional material is available if he knows where to look.

Unfortunately the choice of the best channels of distribution is one that comes low on the list of priorities for many
smaller business owners and managers. Although there is
usually an accepted method of distribution for most products
and services, many firms, if they looked, would discover
alternative channels which may be used in place of the
traditional method, or in addition to it. Too many businesses
get set into the most obvious method when, with a little
imagination they could save expense whilst reaching their
market more intensively, or more selectively(whichever
matches their objectives most closely). The selection of
channels of distribution should form one of the basics
of the marketing plan and, in common with other mar-

keting activities, should be re-examined regularly.

CHANNELS OF DISTRIBUTION

In our look at selling and sales management it soon became apparent that products and services do not sell themselves. Somewhere along the line, each and every product or service has to be sold, either by the manufacturer as in the case of many industrial products, or by relying on somebody else as in the case of most consumer products and services. But contact with customers is only half the battle in making a sale; the other half is making your product or service available to those customers. It doesn't matter how many needs are aroused or customers persuaded, if the goods are not available, forget it.

The function of the channels of distribution is to make products and services available to as many potential customers as possible, and, in most cases, to sell them. Admittedly, the selling function of a self-service supermarket is less intense than that of an insurance broker, but attractive display, comfortable surroundings and persuasive point-of-sale activity are part of the sales process. Because potential customers are normally such a diverse lot and, in the Western world, spoilt for choice, the role of effective distribution is a vital one for all smaller businesses.

Direct to customer

For some industrial suppliers and most consumer companies the option of selling direct to customers is neither a practical nor sensible method of distribution. However, many businesses that deal only with other businesses will find it suits them to deal direct with all their customers. There are also a number of consumer products and services that lend themselves to dealing direct — methods used are: door-to door, mail order, party plan, local advertising, fairs, exhibitions and markets.

Whether you are dealing with industrial customers or final consumers the benefits of direct selling are substantial. If there is a need to demonstrate or explain a complex product or service it may be difficult to find intermediaries with the necessary skills. It is also difficult to control selling activity if it is carried out by intermediaries, they may concentrate on selling competitor's products or services. Another major advantage is the saving of the sometimes considerable profit margins made by intermediaries. The growth of direct selling manufacturers in certain areas of business, such as furniture, is a result of price competition squeezing out the middlemen.

If customers are easily identified, and the product or service of a reasonably high unit value, it may well be worth considering direct distribution. However, the cost of direct selling is high and, even if it is more profitable in terms of gross margin, these profits can quickly disappear on higher marketing expenses. There are many intermediaries with considerable skills and market know-how and there is often a strong argument to let them get on with the selling, leaving the manufacturer to develop the skills he knows best.

The classic wholesale/retail chain

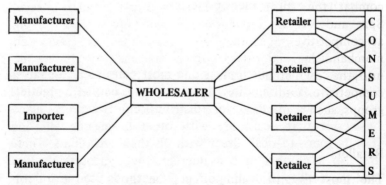

Fig 7.1. The role of the wholesaler

The distribution pattern in Fig 7.1 is a graphic illustration of what an important role the wholesaler can play in the process of getting a large range of products to a great many consumers. In many trades, wholesalers play a vital role breaking large consignments of goods into smaller quantities manageable by retailers. They store goods, set prices and make deliveries; they often have a sales force which is highly specialist and knows a particular geographical area intimately. Fancy goods, clothing and confectionery/tobacco are trades that still depend very much on the traditional wholesaler.

But there are a number of variations offering wholesaling facilities; in the grocery trade, cash and carry warehouses have taken over from the traditional wholesaler. Some of the groups, such as Makro and Nurdin & Peacock are very large organisations and, by buying in quantity and reducing services (like delivery), manage to offer goods to independent retailers at reasonable prices. Distributors perform the same function as wholesalers but tend to specialise in either one type of product or deal with only one manufacturer. The newspaper and magazine publishing industry depends on a relatively small number of specialist distributors.

Another class of wholesale-type operators are the buying groups and co-operatives. These have come from groups of wholesalers or retailers joining forces, for certain activities, to combat the threat from large multiple retailers. Mace, Spar and VG are familiar names and, apart from buying at competitive rates, they offer retail members advice on merchandising and other business matters. Most have gone into the 'own-brand' trade to make their shops even more competitive. Other trades have set up co-operative buying groups, such as electrical goods and clothing.

Retailers

The most essential, and by far the largest, part of the distribution process is retailing. It is difficult to imagine

life without retailers and impossible to consider how any
economy could survive without them. In some trades, retail
groups are now so powerful that they control markets and
dictate to manufacturers; food is a good example where a
small number of supermarket chains control over 50% of a
massive market. These retailers conduct intensive indirect
marketing campaigns and their importance to the suppliers of
goods they sell cannot be overstressed.

Types of retail outlet:

● *Independents*: including small local chains, these are
   mainly served by wholesale outlets and buying groups,
   although the more specialist of them sometimes deal
   direct with manufacturers.

● *Co-op*: although each retailing society operates
   independently, central buying is done through the
   Co-operative Wholesale Societies (CWS). The market
   share of co-operative societies has declined substantially
   over the past few years.

● *Department Stores*: another declining sector of the
   retail market, department stores deal with a vast range
   of products and services. There has been a tendency
   for these stores to amalgamate into chains which take
   on the nature of very widely based multiples. Although
   their buying patterns have tended to remain the same
   (i.e. local buying decision) central approval is normally
   required for particular products and product ranges.

● *Multiples*: the large supermarket chains together with
   specialist units such as Boots, W.H. Smith, Burtons, the
   cash and carry warehouses − Comet, Trident, and a few
   general stores like Marks and Spencer, BHS and
   Woolworths. These all have either central buying or a
   policy of central approval and local decision making.

The smaller business that needs to sell through retailers will have to consider how to get the most exposure for his products and the practicalities of dealing with buyers. Selling to retail and wholesale buyers is somewhat more difficult than selling direct to consumers, they have a greater degree of sophistication and know the market a lot better.

Agents and brokers

In some trades there are specialist brokers and agents through which suppliers will find it better to deal — commodities and financial services are common examples. Some manufacturers use factors who look after warehousing and handling but do not take an active part in marketing the products.

The most common use of agents by smaller businesses is for selling specialist industrial products and exports. A selling agent will work for one or two manufacturers only and get to know the products very well — he may also be likened to a self-employed member of the sales staff. Manufacturers' agents generally work in a limited geographical area calling on a certain type of customer. They will deal with a range of compatible products and services and, as with all agents, derive an income from taking commission from goods sold. A smaller business owner or manager using an agent should ensure that enough effort is being made in selling his product by offering a better deal to the agent than competitors.

CHANNEL SELECTION

The selection of the channels of distribution is a decision that goes right back to the initial objectives set by the business owner or manager. Method of distribution must appear prominently in the short, medium and long-term marketing plans, but continuous efforts must be made to ensure existing distribution is the best available and

to look for new and improved methods. Many businesses fail
to make the most out of their distribution effort and it is
probably the most persistently ill-considered marketing
activity.

The fundamental choice between wanting to skim a
market or to really penetrate it, is one of the most basic
objectives of a business and comes up as a factor in marketing
planning time and time again. Clearly, this decision will very
much influence the type of distribution network that a
business uses. Penetration may be on a limited geographical
area or on a national basis, but means the intensive coverage
of a target market.

On the other hand, many smaller businesses decide that
their main objective is to skim the market by creaming off
the most attractive, most profitable or easiest targets.
Skimming may be achieved by selecting only certain outlets
for a product or service with the result that only certain
elements of a possible market are reached. This selectivity is
most commonly found in the giftware and cosmetics
industries. Price is also a major factor, but the right amount
of selective control can only be made by choosing and using
the right channels of distribution.

The nature of the product or service and the characteristics of the target market are major considerations when
examining channels of distribution. There may be firmly
established channels which demand use — the small magazine
publisher will find life difficult without using one of the
established distributors if the publication is to be sold over
the counter. But he still has several alternative channels to
consider. Magazines may be sent free to a selected list of
readers, relying solely on income from advertising; they may
be sold through subscription by mail order or advertising;
they may be sold at special events or distributed door-
to-door.

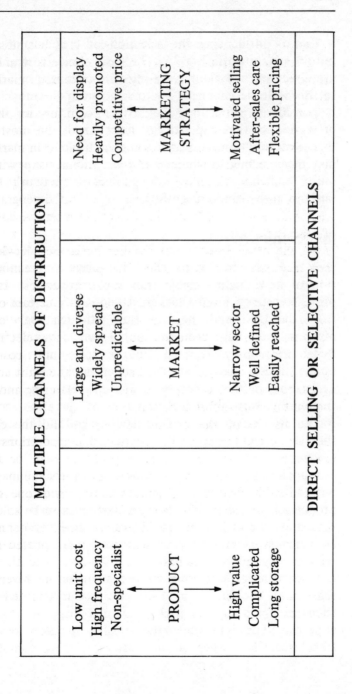

Fig. 7.2. Factors in channel selection

MULTIPLE CHANNELS OF DISTRIBUTION

PRODUCT

Low unit cost
High frequency
Non-specialist

High value
Complicated
Long storage

MARKET

Large and diverse
Widely spread
Unpredictable

Narrow sector
Well defined
Easily reached

MARKETING STRATEGY

Need for display
Heavily promoted
Competitive price

Motivated selling
After-sales care
Flexible pricing

DIRECT SELLING OR SELECTIVE CHANNELS

Factors influencing the selection of channels of distribution are shown in Fig 7.2. The basic choice is whether to use direct selling or only very selective channels, or whether to use multiple channels. Factors shown in the model must be considered in turn and their effect noted, if your product or service, market and strategy meet largely the top group then you will tend towards using multiple channels. This may mean selling to wholesalers *and* national buyers for the multiple chains *and* selling through mail order, all as part of a fairly intensive marketing effort.

FRANCHISING

Over the past few years there has been a virtual explosion of new, highly visible franchise operations — Prontaprint, Kentucky Fried Chicken, Dyno-Rod and many more from the U.K. and the U.S. But, although not quite so obvious, there have been substantial franchise operations in Britain for many years; most of our service stations and many public houses have franchised operations, and exclusive dealerships in the motor trade and cosmetics are forms of franchising. But in the U.S. this type of operation accounts for an even larger share of all retailing and all the signs are that the growth there will be repeated here over the next few years.

Franchising offers many opportunities for people who wish to enter business for themselves by providing less-risky propositions than if they were to start from scratch. At the same time the technique provides established businesses with the means to expand and distribute their products and services on a much wider basis.

Essentially, a franchise is an agreement for one business to sell, on an exclusive basis, another's products or services in exchange for a support package of marketing and business expertise. The franchisee (the smaller operator) pays the franchisor (the owner of the business idea) a commission or royalty payment and usually an initial fee for setting up costs. Exclusive dealerships and other licences to sell or use a trade name are similar, but here we will examine the form known as 'modern franchising'.

The franchisee is an independent business operator, he owns the equipment, buys the stock, keeps the goodwill and owns or rents the premises. The franchisor owns the business idea and the trading style and the contract made between them will make their respective statuses clear. Also in the contract will be the granting of a licence and it will set out the terms of royalty and other payments.

Although agreements differ, the franchisor will normally undertake national and local advertising and sales promotion, provide full training for the franchisee and his staff, will provide an element of exclusivity and give a certain amount of administrative and business support. The franchisor may help with finance and will take an active part in setting up the business and work until it is running smoothly.

There are many advantages to the franchisee. There is considerably less risk as the business idea is already tried and tested and the methods of business operation and marketing will be firmly established. The franchisee will benefit from bulk-buying discounts and the knowledge and negotiating skills of the franchisor. The franchisor offers detailed market information and the benefit of trade marks and patents. The franchisee will normally require lower capital investment than if he tried to establish a new business from scratch.

On the other hand there are disadvantages to operating a franchise. The very nature of the agreement means an element of control which can often go against the nature of the entrepreneurial spirit needed by anyone in business. The franchisee will have to pay the fees out of profits, which inevitably means lower profitability (but not necessarily lower income) and the franchisee may be unable to effect better profits by buying supplies elsewhere. The franchisor may have an adverse influence on the franchisee's income through bad decisions or policy. Finally, the contract may have an increasingly limiting effect on the franchisee as his business expands, and many franchise arrangements come under severe strain if the franchisee is particularly successful.

EXPORTING

Overseas markets can provide businesses with new opportunities to increase their sales and to make larger profits. Indeed many smaller businesses in the U.K. export a large proportion of their outputs and successfully carry the flag in the most surprising places. But there are many dangers, not the least of these being expensive failure. Marketing for export is not merely transferring one's marketing efforts to other countries; it requires a different approach and a quite separate structure.

Choosing the right markets and researching them are major problems; the government, through the British Overseas Trade Board offers plenty of help, but there is no substitute for first-hand contact. There is considerable demand overseas for certain British products and services – high technology, craftwork and high quality goods. But, as with all marketing, effective distribution is the key to effective exporting and the smaller business will need help.

The option of setting up a company-owned sales and distribution network around the world, or even in Europe, is not really a practical one for any smaller business. But physically getting the goods to export markets and contact with potential customers are activities that cannot be avoided. Some firms operate mail order by advertising in appropriate local publications and then using the post to deliver the goods; published material is often marketed overseas in this way.

More often than not, direct selling through the mail is not possible and the business owner will have to depend on local distributors and agents to sell for him. Sometimes home based export merchants may be used as a first step — they have established contacts and will normally deal with a particular industry or trade. More usually, local agents will have to be found in each country of export. Finding suitable agents is difficult and, again, help is available from the government through the BOTB and through local Embassies and Consulates.

The businessman will need to think very carefully before exporting. Sales literature and other promotional material will need redesigning and *must* be written in the appropriate language. The name of the product will have to be tested in each language — it may be completely inappropriate. And the business will get involved in trade fairs and exhibitions and other special promotional efforts. This activity takes time and resources, but Britain is a great trading nation and there are many opportunities, and profitable ones, waiting for the entrepreneur.

DISTRIBUTION

CHECKLIST

1 Can you identify exactly which channels of distribution you use for each of your products or services?
2 Have you considered other channels and tested their suitability?
3 If you use agents, are you sure that they are putting sufficient effort into selling your products or services?
4 Are there established channels of distribution for your trade or industry? If so do you use them without any thought for trying other channels?
5 Are you skimming or penetrating the market and does your distribution policy reflect your objectives?
6 Have you considered the market, product and strategy influences on your business and does your distribution policy reflect these influences?
7 Have your considered franchising your business idea?
8 Have you considered extending your business by taking on a franchise operation?
9 Have you considered widening your market by exporting?
10 If you already export, are you aiming your efforts at the best and most profitable markets?
11 If you already export, have you re-assessed your marketing operation recently and considered the effectiveness of your distributors and agents?

8
Retail Marketing

Retailers provide the business world with the most effective means of presenting products to the millions of consumers that make up any civilised society. They also provide customers with the opportunity to select from the many competitive items on offer and to exercise choice as to where they spend their limited resources. Shops and other retail outlets form the most significant part of the marketing network and as such deserve special recognition from all those engaged in marketing. Acting as they are, constantly under the critical scrutiny of the consumer, retailers must be particularly careful in anything they do. All management decisions can be directly translated into the effect they have on the customer and should consequently be seen as marketing decisions.

Retailers are businesses in their own right and will profit from applying sound marketing techniques to their day to day operation. This involves acceptance of marketing principles, awareness of the market around them, and the implementation of good marketing management. Retailers have a need for planning, and like all businesses must always be aware of the profitability of their activities, as a whole and each individual element. Creative marketing is essential to attract the maximum number of customers and to generate sufficient goodwill to keep those customers — more than any other type of business, the retailer depends on repeat sales.

The premises chosen, where they are situated, the layout, and upkeep will profoundly effect the level of business achieved by any retail outlet. A shop must be stocked; not at random, but with a balanced selection of the right products at the right price, and they must be effectively displayed. Stock control is vital. A retailer cannot afford to have too much stock lying around the place, but it is indefensible to sell out of a product that is in demand.

Even the best retail outlets could not claim that, because they are there, stock sells itself. Similarly, although manufacturers and major distributors spend vast resources promoting their products, this is still not enough. Retailers must promote their own businesses and must take positive action to maximise their sales. Staff should be presentable and trained in the art of salesmanship, ready to exploit any sales opportunity. Point-of-sale and in-store promotions must be attractive and window displays should invite customers to look around. Local advertising and good public relations are part and parcel of retail management.

Recent trends in retailing; the growth of franchising, mail order, and supermarketing have inflicted their toll on the small independent retailer. But effective marketing need not cost a fortune and will equip the retailer to respond to the challenges of competition and prepare him to face changes in buying habits. We are bound to see many more developments in retailing over the next few years, but with a basis of sound marketing practice the retailer will be ready.

CUSTOMERS

Satisfied customers become regular customers, and regular customers provide retailers with their main sources of business. They provide a reliable income, which is the bread and butter of any retailer's turnover − impulse and walk-in customers are only the jam. Regular customers are easier to sell to, they recommend the business to their friends and acquaintances and help generally to raise goodwill. Maintaining good customer relations must be the long-term marketing objective of every retail operation.

All the rules and guidelines given in this book apply as much to retailers as to any other types of business. A systematic, organised and planned approach to marketing, over an extended period of time, is the only base upon which a retail business may successfully develop. But retailers do have some special problems and this chapter will identify these and help to deal with them.

Retailing is essentially a service; a service to the public at large, and a service to manufacturing and importing businesses. A good retail owner or manager will have to look after both. But marketing is about customers, and the first principle of marketing is certainly the first rule of retailing — start with the customers and base your efforts on their requirements, not your own aspirations and beliefs. 'The customer is always right' is a cliché-ed phrase, but one that is as true now as it was in Dickens' time, when grovelling seemed to be the order of the day.

Under the massive competitive forces of the large supermarket chains, the question must be asked: How come there are thousands and thousands of small independent food shops, charging considerably more for the same products, still in existence? The simple one-word answer is *service!* They are open longer, some deliver and some offer credit, and they all give personal attention to customers.

To maintain good customer relations (and consequently keep its customers), the retail business must comply with a few simple terms of reference, some essential to all businesses and some optional, depending on the circumstances. But retailers, who are very much at the 'sharp end' of the marketing process, must *always* think of their customers first and must devote their attention to projecting and maintaining the best possible relationship with the buying public.

Basic rules of an effective customer policy:

- Operate with a planned long-term marketing strategy
- Always offer a fair deal (not necessarily the cheapest)
- Provide a personal attention package with —
  - an adequate number of well-trained staff
  - a pleasant and friendly atmosphere
  - a reasonable complaints/returns procedure
- Offer customers a range of services (depending on the trade)
  - credit facilities
  - delivery/installation
  - after-sales care
  - repair facilities
  - fast response to orders
  - utilities (toilets, telephone, changing rooms, etc)

Some elements of customer policy are there for all to follow, and some are necessary for particular trades. Washing machines need installing, and the smaller retailer may beat the big cash and carry warehouses on this point. Dress shops will have to provide changing facilities and mirrors, and restaurants should provide toilet and washing facilities. If it is necessary to provide utilities, make sure they are in good condition, and work properly — an out-of-order telephone can do more damage than having no telephone at all.

Other aspects of customer policy are optional and the use of them by the retailer will depend on a number of factors. Remember that the purpose of providing services is to attract custom away from competitors (direct and indirect) in order to make higher profits. Offering services only to find that their overhead costs far exceed any benefits to income or profitability is not only a waste of resources, but stupid. The retailer must carefully gauge the marginal benefits of each new or existing service offered based on estimates of increased or lost sales using the following principles.

Take the example that a nearby competitor has installed a new repair workshop to offer same-day repair facilities, previously you had both sent repairs away which took at least several days to return. You are faced with the decision of whether or not to establish your own repair facilities. (These calculations work for any service or if you wish to extend your range by introducing a new product line).

Establish the following figures: (all based on one full year)

a — Estimated increased sales if service installed
b — Estimated lost sales if service not installed
c — Total cost of establishing the service
d — Gross profit (margin) per sale
e — Total net profits

Any one of four situations will apply.

1 $(a \times d) > c$
If new income is greater than the cost of installing the service it should be installed.

2 $(b \times d) > c - (a \times d)$
If the cost of installation is greater than new income, but this is still less than lost income, the service should be installed and efforts made to increase profitability.

3 $c - (a \times d) > (b \times d)$
If the cost is greater than new income and the net cost greater than lost income, the service should not be installed and attention given to different methods of increasing business and profitability.

4 $c - (a \times d) > (b \times d) > e$
If lost income is less than net cost but is greater than

total net profits, it may still be worth installing the service just to save the business, but urgent consideration must be given to other methods of increasing business and profitability.

SELLING AND SALES STAFF

The art of salesmanship in retail stores is not lost, only difficult to find. This is a great pity as active selling is as important to the retail store as the Post Office is to mail order retailers. One look at the U.S., at the courtesy generally shown to all customers and the persuasiveness of the selling in almost every store, quickly shows why the American retail sector is so much healthier than its British equivalent. All the rules of selling apply to shop staff, who have a considerable advantage over other salesmen – the customers come to them and indicate an interest in the product or service they wish to buy. How industrial salesmen would love that to happen!

Retail selling is part of a marketing package which includes a whole range of activities – merchandising, point-of-sale display, stock control, outside promotion and customer service, and, with the not inconsiderable exception of self-service, provides the most important part of the process. But all too often, retail owners and managers fail to recruit the right people, fail to train them, and lose plenty of business for their lack of effort in this area.

The need for training is great – selling is a difficult job, but one that is learnt and, more importantly, developed over a period of time. Initial training can be provided by commercial schools or by colleges and the Distributive Industries Training Board – all sales staff should be given initial training and then provided with regular on-the-job development training. Without acquiring the skills nobody can be expected to perform well in such a difficult job as selling.

Sales staff require a number of attributes which should

be reflected in the type of person recruited. They will require a good understanding of the product: How many sales have been lost because a sales assistant hasn't a clue about electronics, German wines or modern poetry? The personality and attitudes required in serving customers are just as important. An ideal salesman will be polite and good-humoured, speak articulately (and appropriately), will be confident and presentable. The salesman will have a positive attitude towards the job and should be in good health. A tall order but one that should be met whenever possible.

Selling should be planned and reference made to the sales process (see Chapter 6), because to make a sale the customer will have to be taken along a logical process to the final close. The customer's confidence will have to be won − in the salesman, the goods and in the establishment, and his needs established. As with all selling, the customer will raise objections which have to be overcome gently but firmly. Often in a retail situation the customer will have a choice right up to the close, and the salesman will have to help the customer make this choice by reducing dissonance − the conflict in the customer's mind between choices and the fear of making the wrong decision. The salesman will need to have an eye towards maximising the value of the sale, and finally make the close.

Retailers depend on repeat business and sometimes the line between competent and effective selling, and sharp practice is thin. No retailer can afford the accusation of sharp practice − the secret of a successful operation is to *always* offer a fair and reasonable deal. It doesn't have to be the cheapest, if it did there would only be one supplier of everything. But if a customer feels he has been cheated, not only will the store never see him again, but it won't see any of his friends.

STORE MANAGEMENT

There is not a lot of point in opening up a retail operation if there is insufficient sales potential at the location. This does not just mean numbers of people, but numbers of the right people who are willing and able to visit those particular premises. There may be tens of thousands of adults living in a northern industrial town — but there won't be many of them wanting to travel one mile out of town to rent a dinner suit. Likewise, there are not a lot of fish and chip shops in the City of London (although there are plenty in the suburbs).

Before opening a retail store a business owner or manager must carry out some marketing research. The market — a definition, its size, distribution and purchasing power, is it likely to grow or is it declining and what is the population profile. The competition — where it is, how it operates, whether it has plans for expansion and how it will react to a new store. Operational — product range, method of trading (self-service, cash and carry), security, resources required for setting up, pedestrian traffic, parking and pricing policy. Results of this research will indicate the optimum location and the action required to operate profitably.

Once the location has been established and the premises taken, the business owner or manager will decide the manner in which the store will operate. Premises, together with staff, stock, equipment and his own enterprise are the means for him to carry out his business, but marketing policy will determine how efficiently those means are used. The initial internal consideration is in-store *customer traffic flow*. Some premises will dictate how people will use the store, but in most cases the owner or manager will be able to influence the flow and use it to his advantage. It is also important to consider the long-term effects of appearance on the general image of the business which must be accommodated whatever the short-term expedient of maximum exposure of stock to customer flow.

Almost all retail stores now have an element of self-selection, the exceptions are those trading in very small, high priced items such as jewellery and cigarettes. Self-selection, and of course its big brother, self-service, puts a premium on good store layout. As much of the stock (or range of stock) as possible should be put in front of the customer who must also be able to inspect and, in most cases, handle it. There is a permanent conflict between the need for attractive display, which uses a lot of valuable space, and the need to exhibit the maximum amount of stock. The only answer is to use common sense coupled with experiment; be continually on the lookout for more efficient display methods and spend some of your spare time on a little marketing research in your competitor's stores.

Effective layout directs customers past (even only with their eyes) a logical arrangement of merchandise in order to obtain the maximum sales per square metre of display area. But not just any old sales, the retail owner or manager will have some lines that are more profitable than others and customers should be drawn to them. The most profitable items are rarely those most in demand so the owner will also have to take into consideration volume of sales as well as the mark-up of individual lines. Customer flow will depend on three basic elements:

● Physical layout of equipment;
● Positioning of high-demand items;
● Effect of promotional material.

Equipment such as counters and display units must never appear to act as a barrier to the customer, they must be placed along the main customer routes and not across them. Placing items in highest demand at the far end of the routes will help direct customers past other products which may be displayed on the way. However this could have a harmful side-effect in that it may cause irritation through sheer inconvenience. Customer convenience may mean that high-frequency purchase items should be placed near to the entrance and close to sales assistance — the owner may have to consider other means of highlighting a wider range of stock if this is the case. Judicious use of display aids and lighting may attract attention to where it is most needed.

Whatever style of trading is adopted it must not be forgotten that this is a competitive age and all retail owners and managers will do much better if they employ good salesmanship as an integral part of their operations. While staff should not pester customers, who should feel free and relaxed and able to look around, they should always be there to help, encourage and persuade. Nothing is worse for a customer than to feel ignored, the very fact that he or she is in the store means an interest in a purchase and questions that require answers, and there are many hundreds of sales lost because inattentive staff are gossiping to each other rather than dealing with customers and selling goods.

Merchandising is the front end of stock control and simply means ensuring adequate quantities of stock items are on display to the public. As with all stock control activities, to operate an effective merchandising policy the retailer must equip himself with certain information.

- Current stock levels of all items
- What items have been sold
- The average rate at which each item sells
- Seasonal or unusual demand patterns
- Best price for each individual item

A system must be created that allows this information to be generated and control maintained. Products will generally only sell if they are displayed — to sell out of something, except because of supply difficulties, is an unforgiveable error, but to lose a sale because an item which is sitting in the stockroom is not on display is a gross and heinous crime of commerce.

PROMOTIONAL ACTIVITY

Retail advertising is the fastest growing sector in almost all media, the large multiple chains spend many millions on television and newspaper advertising, and the local press is stuffed with ads for local retail operations. But space and time in the media is only one aspect of retail promotional activity: door-to-door leaflets, mail shots, special events and point-of-sale display are all used to great effect by the retail operator. Essentially, all the rules that are discussed in the following chapters apply as much to retailers as to any other business and efforts should be made both to indirectly sell particular items or groups of items, and to lift the image of the business in general.

As with all marketing activity retail promotions must be planned and offer consistency. Promotions will often be tied to a particular product or range which will have distinctive features; one or two of these features should be taken as the theme of the promotion and reflected in each part. For example, a new range of British bicycles might be on offer, the Britishness may well be the best feature and this message should be repeated in advertisements, on leaflets, on window posters and on point-of-sale material. To say on one that they are British, on another that they are cheap and another that they are rugged will only serve to dilute the message and confuse potential customers.

Other promotions will be based on a particular event: Christmas, the summer, a clearance sale or the Pope's visit. These are convenient 'handles' on which to attach promotional effort and again a consistent message must be clearly put across. The main point to watch with special events is that the offer is credible and relevant – the 'Closing Down Sale' wears a bit thin after several months, and a new power drill doesn't really make a suitable Mother's Day gift.

Many manufacturers produce point-of-sale aids such as display units and signs. Care must be taken in the use of this material as good visual display can easily turn into clutter. It is better to single out a particular theme and push that for a period of time, moving on to another theme at an appropriate time. The big department stores are particularly good at this technique but there is no reason why even the smallest outlet cannot adopt the principle to great effect. Special purchases may be made and manufacturers asked for material and other assistance; in some cases Trade Associations run thematic programmes like Children's Book Week and Sausage Week.

The object of promotional activity is to increase sales *and* profits; there is not much point in promoting more sales if the cost of the promotional activity is higher than the profit derived from it. The retailer must budget carefully all promotional expenditure and monitor its effect. A new glossy catalogue may be very good for the ego, but if it does not bring in the results, and does little to build the image of the business, then the expenditure should be directed elsewhere. The merchandise itself is often the most effective and cheapest promotional aid and a good window display is well worth a generous chunk of the promotional budget.

RETAIL MARKETING

CHECKLIST

1 Do you have a planned customer relations policy?
2 Do you make a positive effort to establish the needs of your customers and try to meet them?
3 Do you always offer a fair deal?
4 Have you examined the services you offer your customers and do they pay? Are there any others you could introduce that will increase your business profitability?
5 Have you a written job description for your sales staff, if so do you recruit to it?
6 Do you provide initial and development training for your staff?
7 Have you considered how your layout affects customer traffic flow? Could you improve sales by changing the layout of your store?
8 Do high--profit items receive adequate exposure?
9 Have you an operational system providing all the information necessary for an effective merchandising and stock control programme?
10 Do you plan your promotional activity well in advance?
11 Is your promotional activity profitable?
12 Do you rotate your displays on a thematic basis?
13 How inviting is your window display?

PART IV
Advertising
&
Sales
Promotion

9
Above the Line

Few people would dispute the profound effect advertising has had on the western world; a trip behind the Iron Curtain soon shows how dull life is without it — in Britain, advertising is a multi-million pound business without which the media could not survive. The expression 'above the line' refers to paid advertising, space booked in all forms of the media, as opposed to other types of promotional activity dealt with in later chapters.

With time on television measured in thousands of pounds, advertising can be unbelievably expensive. On the other hand a small lineage advertisement placed in the local newspaper will cost only a few pounds. But, whatever the expenditure, advertising must always be made to work and meet the objectives of the advertiser. There is little point in advertising without first establishing the role it has to play within the overall marketing plan.

While most advertising is informative in nature, it must not be assumed that, because of this, it should not also be persuasive. There is a difference between advertising that informs and that designed to generate an active response, but the purpose of all advertising is to persuade somebody to do something; at one end to adopt a favourable attitude towards a business as a corporate body, and at the other to send off an order.

An advertiser may wish to announce a new product or to remind customers of an existing one. This information may be aimed at end users, consumer or industrial, or at wholesalers, retailers and other middle-men. Information may refer to price changes, alterations in specification, new uses for products, special offers, or to reinforce brands. Whatever the case, the advertiser does not necessarily expect the customer to do anything at the time he reads the advertisement but does hope to influence a later buying decision.

For a number of businesses, advertising provides the best or only way to <u>sell</u> to their customers. This is especially true where a market is large and diverse and the unit price of the product or service relatively low. The part that advertising plays in this selling process may be to evoke a buying decision (as in the case of mail order), or to generate enquiries to be followed up later. The objective of this type of advertising is to obtain a specific response which can be measured and monitored.

The range of media is almost overwhelming: commercial radio, cinema, television, and telephone directories, for example, each offer different opportunities to the advertiser. Newspapers and magazines usually rely heavily on advertising for their revenue, and for some it is the only source of income. There are hoardings and posters everywhere: on the roadways and railways, in taxis, buses, trains; at football grounds and airports. Selection is a most difficult process and success can only come with careful study and experimentation.

Advertising agencies function as go-betweens for advertisers and media owners. Agencies are specialists in planning, creating, and placing advertisements and in assisting businesses with other aspects of their creative marketing activities. They will provide artists and copywriters and give expert help in analysing media opportunities. As agencies derive the bulk of their income from commission paid by media owners (commission <u>not</u> paid to firms that book advertising space direct) their services come cheaply to the advertiser. With professionalism in advertising so important for effective results, all businesses should use an agency if possible.

TYPES OF ADVERTISING

It is an unfortunate truth that many businesses do not recognise the full value of advertising until they are failing through lack of exposure and a consequent shortage of customers. Similarly, in hard times advertising is often the first thing to go; just when it is needed most. If you are proud of your business and want to see it survive and prosper — advertise. Constantly!

It is never enough just to advertise once or when the feeling takes you, and then sit back and wait for the customers to flock in through your doors for ever more. The general public is fickle, forgetful and has plenty of choice; customers need to be reminded frequently of who you are and what you have to offer.

There are several basic types of above-the-line advertising:

Display advertisements do just that — they display goods or services in an eye-catching style to generate interest or a desire to purchase. Display advertisements appear throughout the body of the publication in either black-and-white or colour. Special positions such as front or back covers are available at a premium charge above the basic advertising rate. They may be large or small and the key to success lies in good design; easy to understand and easy on the eye. They must provide all the basic information the potential customer needs: price, supplier, outlet location, availability, etc. — and of course details of the product or service itself. Rates are based on cost per single column centimetre although there will be standard charges for standard sizes such as whole-page and half-page.

Classified advertisements usually appear towards the back of any publication, generally under a large 'Classified' heading. The rates in classified sections are usually substantially higher than for display advertising because of the extra work involved for the publisher in handling the 'small ads' that appear in this section. Similar interest advertisements are usually grouped together: cars, business services and restaurants for example. This can work for or against the advertiser. There may be a danger of 'swamping' but, on the other hand, there are benefits in being easy to find and identify. Some publications are composed entirely of classified advertising, for example: *Exchange and Mart, Dalton's Weekly* and *Yellow Pages*. A classified advertisement need not be a small one; the term simply refers to the fact that the advertisement has been classified into a section. Huge recruitment advertisements in the national press may still be classified.

Semi-Display advertisements fall somewhere between full display and classified. They are in display format but are simply too small to appear in the main body of the publication because the publication has a policy not to accept a display advertisement below a certain size. Semi-display advertisements must be particularly well designed and clear since they may suffer from their smallness and the swamping effect. For convenience, publishers frequently group particular sizes of semi-display advertisements together (regardless of classification) in or near the full classified section. Others make an effort to classify by size and category. Prices of semi-display are usually between full display and classified rates.

Feature advertisements are becoming more and more common. They can be seen particularly in free newspapers and trade magazines, which derive all their income from advertising. Relevant advertisers are encouraged to advertise *en bloc* within a whole section of the publication in which the editorial is devoted to one subject: gardening, Winchester, holidays, for example. The incentives to the advertiser are usually a favourable advertising rate and a possible editorial mention.

Local commercial radio has its equivalent of display and classified advertising, with equivalent rate structures. Radio advertisers usually book a series of short slots and, like premium position advertising in publications, peak-time radio exposure is more expensive than off-peak. Offering tremendous flexibility, the choice of advertising style for radio is entirely up to the advertiser: jingle, announcement or constructed conversation can all be very effective.

Commercial television advertising is very expensive and the high costs of studio and production time usually put it out of the reach of most smaller businesses — but not always. Furniture stores, restaurants and other smaller companies can do well by advertising on local stations where they reach a mass audience.

One other type of advertisement is in common use by advertisers, large and small. This is the paid insert — a leaflet that is inserted in a publication and mailed, or sold over the counter, to the full readership or a geographical part of it. An insert has the advantage of being easily spotted and the disadvantage of being easily thrown away, but it is particularly useful for direct response advertisers as there is a built in reluctance on the part of readers to cut up their publications.

Advertising styles have developed over the years, to the stage that they are now an art form of their own — consider the obtuse but picturesque cigarette advertisements in the weekend colour supplements, or radio and television jingles that turn into pop songs. But one thing is certain, each advertisement must be designed to suit the chosen medium. And, in the words of the Advertising Standards Authority, advertisements must be: 'Legal, Truthful, Honest and Decent'.

INFORMATION OR RESPONSE?

Before contemplating the specific design of an advertisement, it must be decided for what purpose it is being created. A mail order business has one simple objective for its advertising — to sell products and services quickly and efficiently. A high technology business, however, is unlikely to sell expensive goods on the strength of one single advertisement. It must embark on a planned marketing campaign with advertising designed to create awareness of the product, encourage acceptance of the product and to promote applications of the product, leaving it to the highly experienced and knowledgeable salesman to close the actual sale.

So advertisements can either solicit a specific and *active response* or offer *information*. In practice all advertising is response advertising to some extent — the only truly informative advertisements are those placed by government or public bodies and even these are designed also to create a better attitude towards that government or body. But for our purposes we must decide where the emphasis lies and what response is expected.

Action in response to advertising may be direct and immediate (mail order again), or indirect and delayed (persuading a housewife to adopt a favourable attitude to solid fuel). But even active response advertisements will not necessarily produce an immediate sale. Potential customers may send for literature, free samples or test drive, but it will probably be a salesman who finally 'sells' the product. This is particularly true of the more expensive items: cars, hi-fi and furniture for example.

A well designed active response advertisement will motivate the potential customer to actually do something by including incentive. Incentive may come in the form of a time factor, such as a limited period 'special offer', it may be a price reduction, money-off coupon to the first 500 applicants, or even a free gift to every customer ordering before a certain date. The general money-off coupon is being used more and more by the large consumer goods companies as it offers incentive to customers and helps the company to monitor the effect of its advertising. The same system can be successfully employed by the smaller business — a new hairdressing salon for example may find it worthwhile to use coupon advertising in local newspapers to attract initial clientele.

Most active response is based on the premise that there is already a demand for the product or service on offer, although customers can also be stimulated into the buying mood for goods they have not previously considered by the judicious use of response advertising. The great advantage, especially to the smaller advertiser, is that the response can be accurately measured — products and creative techniques can be tested — allowing the advertiser to develop the most effective methods.

Delayed response advertising is much more subjective although must also eventually lead to increased sales. For many businesses, this kind of advertising is all that is available because their product or service does not lend itself to active response advertising. People only use a plumber when they need one and do not buy a new car on the strength of advertising alone. Here the potential customer must be wooed from competitors, must be given all the necessary information and have a full explanation of the particular merits of your product or service. When the customer comes forward, or is flushed out by other marketing activities, he must come to your company and if effective, your advertising will have completed much of the sales process in advance. (see Chapter 5 – Sales Process)

PRODUCING AN EFFECTIVE ADVERTISEMENT

An advertisement is quite often the first step towards making a sale (or, as we have seen, the only step). This means that the message in the form of words (copy) and design (layout) are vitally important. Visual embellishments such as line drawings, pictures of glamourous girls, photographs and cartoons serve to catch the eye of the reader and together with the copy persuade him or her to respond. The advertisement must invoke something in the reader – even if only to reinforce a company or trade name.

The headline of an advertisement is paramount, for this is where the message begins. Although hackneyed, there is no doubting the success of key words such as 'Sale', 'Bargain', 'Reduced', 'Clearance' and 'Offer'. Everyone loves a bargain of some sort and statements like 'Was £20 – Now only £16.99' can be extremely effective. Very little more needs to be said (other than product information, when and where) if the product is established and well known. For less price-sensitive items the headline should be concise and informative and capture the imagination of the reader.

Advertising copy must be accurate, informative and effective in the message it is trying to convey. It is the basic explanation of the product or service together with technical details and specifications where necessary. It is important not to include too much information, the reader will get turned-off and quite possibly confused. Remember that most readers consider advertising copy as optional reading and will 'opt out' given the slightest excuse. However, details of products and services not pictured in the advertisement may sometimes be included.

Body copy itself is a selling message, together with graphics and headlines, but the advertisement should lead logically to some form of response stimulation. A 'closer' should appear telling the customer what to do next (at least what you would like him to do). Closers also benefit from key words: 'Last few days', 'Hurry', 'While stocks last', 'Free', 'Send for free illustrated brochure Now'.

Even the very best designed and worded advertisement will fail if the reader/potential customer is unable to identify easily the source of supply, its location and when he should act. Ensure that your company name and logo (you should have one) are clearly featured, together with address (and branches if you have them) as well as telephone numbers. Premises that encourage visitors must also include opening and closing times and brief directions if necessary. It is also a good idea to include which credit cards you accept, especially retailers, or if you don't accept credit cards, say so. Embarrassing moments and lost sales can occur if the customer arrives with no alternative means of payment.

Design is a matter of personal preference but *must*, repeat *must*, look professional and in keeping with the general image of the business. Any business that is engaged in all but the very occasional advertising should use an agency, if not, then be very careful as to the wording, and get several people to read it *before* it appears in print. Media owners will always help with layout and design but do not expect any great creative work, that can only come from the professionals. Do try and include some graphics, pictures and cartoons (watch out for copyright) and interesting typefaces. Even if you do not use an agency it is worthwhile to find a local graphic artist to assist with layout and design. As we have mentioned above, the use of coupons is an excellent idea if at all possible, either for people to send for further details, or to cut out and present at the time of purchase.

RANGE AND CHOICE OF MEDIA

A dazzling array of advertising media is currently available to any business: local and national press; trade journals; consumer magazines; inserts; posters; radio, television and cinema; directories and many more. Because of the choice, the best place to start is to examine the advantages and disadvantages of the main groups of media.

	Advantages	Disadvantages
Local Press	Large localised circulation Frequency and immediacy Relatively cheap Can be booked quickly Cheap production	Non-specific readership Lack of colour
National press	Large circulation Can be booked quickly Cheap production	Non-specific readership Very expensive Short life Lack of colour (or expensive
Consumer magazines	Large circulation Pass-on readership Colour available Relatively long life	Expensive Distant copy dates Swamping by large company expensive advertising
Specialist trade journals	Identifiable readership Can be booked quickly Reader enquiry service Relatively cheap	Highly competitive and danger of swamping by advertising in same field Critical readership

Inserts	Relatively cheap Good for direct response Easily directed	Short life High production costs
Posters	High impact Large readership Relatively cheap Fairly long life Good for reminders	Brief exposure Limited message, ex- cept on transport Not suitable for un- known or 'difficult' products
Directories	Relatively cheap Long life Constant source of new customers	Restricted size and limited message Not eye catching Can be swamped Infrequent and slow in publishing
Commercial radio	Large audience Localised audience Can be directed	Short life and message Expensive pro- duction
Television	Massive coverage Colour, movement and sound	Very expensive time Short life Very expensive production
Cinema	Relatively cheap time Frequent exposure Colour, movement and sound	Expensive produc- tion Audience profile very narrow — the young

Successful advertising depends on the dynamic projection of the product or service in relevant media, reaching the right audience at the best time. Local newspapers offer immediacy and advertisements can appear quickly after they have been booked; generally within a few days, or even hours in exceptional circumstances. As timing of the appearance of an advertisement is so critical, you should make sure that you (your agency should know if you use one) have all the final copy deadlines for each appropriate publication that you are likely to use.

The immediate local press, while being the most suitable for many smaller businesses, is not right for all trades — those trading nationally or involved in a specialist field. These businesses will require either the widest possible coverage or a clearly defined one. The list of advantages and disadvantages should provide a basic guide but the advertiser should: establish the readership claimed by the publications under consideration (these should be supported by ABC audit figures) and the cost for equivalent space; then work out the cost per thousand readers of each comparable publication. This will give a further indication of which is best to use, but beware, the *cheapest is not always the best*. The quality of readership, quality of editorial and quality of circulation all influence the final response rate. Only careful monitoring and experience will show which is the best (another reason for using a good agency).

Each publication will have a circulation manager, or somebody responsible for circulation, who is able to provide details of readership type and number as well as a geographical breakdown of the figures on request. The advertisement manager will provide a rate card on request — this will give full details of the advertising rate structure and mechanical data on column widths, colour and artwork requirements. This information may be used to give a better idea of where to advertise but only careful planning and testing will bring in maximum results.

ADVERTISING AGENCIES

There are many benefits to be derived from the appointment of a suitable advertising agency, not the least of which is that a good agency will have much more expertise – creative, media and back-up – than any company, except the very largest, could possibly afford. Even among large companies there are very few that do not use an agency. However, the appointment of an agency is one of the major stepping stones in the marketing activities of a developing business, and not one to take lightly. Selection must be carefully considered, not rushed and systematically approached.

1 *Identify* a small group of advertising agencies which seem to operate in the right area of interest. Use the *British Rate and Data Advertising Agency List* (national and provincial listings are available) or one of the other many agency listings available at your local library.

2 *Write* to the managing directors of each agency on your list providing information on the size and type of your business, the field in which it operates, your basic objectives and, most important, an indication of your estimated advertising budget for the next year or two. Ask the agency to contact you with a view to setting up a meeting. Abandon any agency that doesn't come back to you within two weeks.

3 When contact has been established, either by phone or letter, arrange *meetings* at either your premises, or preferably, theirs, or both. It is best for both parties to assess each other on 'home' territory before any contract is signed.

4 At the agency, make sure you see and meet the *account executive* who will be looking after your business, and that you meet the creative staff who will be producing

your advertisements. Select a *short-list* and ask each to make a presentation.

5 See *examples* of work each short-listed agency has produced for other clients of similar budgets to your own. Agencies tend to show off impressive pieces of work they have done for big spending clients, so make sure that they know how to accommodate a smaller client. Make sure that the one you choose understands your product or service and your basic proposition in the presentation it makes to you.

6 *Select* which agency suits you best on the strength of what you have seen as well as personalities, creative ability and accessibility. It can be useful, though not essential, to have your agency fairly close to hand. You will have to approve every piece of work it produces and in the early days there will be frequent discussion meetings.

7 Having selected an advertising agency, provide it with a detailed *brief* containing as much of your company's background as possible, together with details of the products or services and customers. Say what you want to achieve. This document is vitally important — it is an accepted fact that an agency is only as good as its brief. State the facts, do not over-estimate, do not conceal necessary information and do not misrepresent your business — the agency may embark on an expensive but totally useless, even damaging, campaign.

8 Establish a good *working relationship* with your agency. Do not let it dominate you but, on the other hand, remember that you employed the agency to provide the expertise and experience to help you to marketing success. If you feel you can do it better yourself, then do so. The hard facts are that the results will show whether the advertising agency has been a success or not.

9 *Development* of the relationship between advertising agency and client is vital, stagnation means redundant ideas. As you become more successful the agency must be capable of growing with you. Clients frequently outgrow their agencies; the reverse often happens too.

10 Businesses rarely stay with one agency for more than a few years. Agencies tend to run out of original ideas, especially when the company has only a small and static range. *Changing* your agency from time to time is almost certainly a good idea, it should inject new impetus and a fresh approach. Remember also that an agency may 'fire' a client, if it feels it has run out of ideas or if you are a difficult and demanding client they are unable to satisfy. Agencies will never deal with two directly competitive products or services and this factor can and does produce movement of clients.

Advertising agencies make the substantial part of their income from a discount paid by media owners (usually 10% to 15%). They will also charge clients for the creative work they do and for any leaflets, brochures and other items they produce. More and more agencies are also charging a fee for their work and this especially applies to their smaller clients. Even so, the cost to the business is still relatively low and except for the very small advertiser usually represents good value for money. The amount of time spent by a company if it does its own advertising, its lack of creative skill and sketchy knowledge of the media market make the use of an effective advertising agency almost a must.

ABOVE THE LINE

CHECKLIST

1 Have you considered advertising as a way of obtaining direct response to generate sales (or enquiries) of your product or service?
2 Could advertising play a larger role and improve the efficiency of your marketing mix?
3 Can you identify the different types of advertising and the role each could play for your business?
4 If your product or service does not lend itself to being sold through indirect means, just what are your advertising objectives?
5 Do your advertisements provide all the necessary information to achieve your objectives?
6 Do your advertisements include a 'punchy' headline, effective copy, good graphics and a closer?
7 Are you aware of the range of media in which it would be appropriate to advertise your product or service?
8 Can you list the most important media for your business and the cost of reaching a thousand readers in each?
9 Do you monitor and test all your advertisements and media used?
10 Do you use an agency, if not have you considered approaching a number to see what they can do for you?   Are you aware of the best method of approaching agencies?
11 If you do use an agency, is it doing the best possible job for you and have you considered seeing what others may offer?

10
Below the Line

In the jargon of marketing, 'below the line' refers to forms of promotion that do not involve the purchase of space or time in the media; often known as sales promotion, it is the vital link between direct selling of a product or service and the indirect approaches of advertising. Techniques employed may be conveniently divided into two groups: special promotions, to consumers and the trade; and display.

Consumer promotions, as the name suggests, are designed to stimulate action by consumers, usually in the form of a fairly immediate purchase. By definition each promotion effort is short-term and should be designed to achieve specific sales objectives. Examples are: money-off coupons, free samples, 'two-for-one', competitions, and in-store demonstrations. Companies are continually looking for new ideas which are used as a central part of their marketing strategy, often as support for major advertising and sales campaigns.

As with promotion aimed at the consumer, trade promotions must be part of a co-ordinated marketing effort. Salesmen will often visit their distributors armed with special promotions designed to boost their company's sales. The offer of a co-operative advertising scheme, contest for sales staff, special discount or quantity rate terms (for a limited period) is a common enough experience for most retailers and wholesalers. Trade promotions are no less important to businesses selling industrial products to other firms — buyers are only human and whilst they will usually look for the best deal, a bottle of Scotch goes down well at Christmas.

Display is a general term covering all manner of product and point-of-sale promotional material together with demonstration and physical display. Some activities tie in closely with merchandising and packaging and include: posters, stands, price markers, floor bins, window stickers, T-shirts, badges, pens, calenders, diaries, notebooks, etc. Recently there has been a rapid growth in the number and diversity of display materials available to the business owner or marketing manager. New technology has had a great influence, but there is a growing awareness of the value and effectiveness of display promotion. Sponsorship is another area of display promotion that has enjoyed increased popularity in recent years.

Exhibitions and trade fairs provide businesses with an opportunity to display and demonstrate their products and services. There are now exhibitions for almost every specialist area together with a number of general events such as the 'Ideal Home' and 'Business to Business' exhibitions. Although results depend to some extent on the size of display area and on the quality (and therefore cost) of the display material, exhibitions are an excellent way for smaller businesses to compete on an almost even footing with their larger competitors. In the case of exporters, trade fairs are often the only way that a smaller business can effectively reach new customers.

Printed material is generated by every business and should provide an ideal opportunity for promotion. Sadly, many businesses fail to grasp this opportunity and some even use it to promote their competitors! Catalogues, price lists and sales literature are especially important to the firm selling to industrial markets or through the channels of distribution. A basic knowledge of printing and the processes involved is

invaluable to all engaged in marketing and will lead to substantial savings. Good, simple and effective use of language is
a must; there is no excuse ever for producing shoddy printed
material.

USING THE MAIL

Marketers make use of the postal service in two main ways,
Mail Order and *Direct Mail* promotion. Almost all businesses
use the post for some kind of sales promotion, even if it is
only the occasional sales letter to a promising new contact.
But to smaller business owners and managers the post provides one of the most widely used marketing tools, sometimes representing their entire sales effort.

Mail order manifests itself in three distinct forms. Firstly
there is the advertisement (Display or Classified) designed
to stimulate an order which is then fulfilled through the
post. Secondly, the catalogue which is sent by post on a
one-off or regular basis which provides the customer with
a permanent source of supply — this system is not restricted
to the large clothing mills, it is used extensively by industrial suppliers, stamp dealers, pornographic book dealers
and many more. Thirdly, there is the 'Mail Shot' designed
to sell a subscription (e.g. Readers Digest), or a product to
business users and consumers.

The post is often used as a promotional medium to announce special offers, clearance sales or to provide general
information. With the recent large increases in postal charges
there has been a growth in door-to-door deliveries of promotional material, but the principles are just the same.

Using the mail has a number of advantages; it is selective
in that potential customers may be isolated and broken
down into relevant groups. Post is personal and, if addressed
to an individual decision-taker, is hard to ignore. But probably the greatest benefit is that results may be accurately
monitored and evaluated. The growth of micro-chip

technology and new sophisticated printing and mailing equipment makes control simpler to manage.

The biggest problem with using the post is the mailing list — its creation and the continuous effort needed for updating it. The primary source of names and addresses is the company's own records — customers' invoices, salesmen's contacts and correspondence. New or additional listings may be made up from directories (trade and telephone), generated through advertising or rented from list brokers, the names of which can be obtained from the Direct Mail Producers Association in London. If the list is to be used on more than one occasion a storage system must be established which allows simple reproduction of labels and constant revision. If large, regular mailings are planned it may be to your advantage to use a specialist mailing house, details of which may be found in the marketing press and direct mail associations.

The sales letter

It is difficult to imagine any occasion when a sales letter should not be included in any type of mailing. Perhaps a purely informative catalogue or brochure may be sent with just a compliments slip; but even then it is worth taking advantage of the mailing to enclose a sales letter promoting your business in general. The letter should be considered as performing the role of salesman — wording and presentation are crucial and, although practice will improve the quality of sales letters, a number of guidelines will help to produce effective letters.

- Define the objectives of the mail shot clearly in your mind — what you are trying to achieve, what response you hope for and the type of person and business to whom you are writing.

- Get to the point straight away. Arrest the reader's attention and show exactly what that reader is going to get out of the deal — save money, make life easier, become more efficient, etc.

- Try attention-grabbing techniques such as a bold and punchy headline, bright colours or specially designed folds that arouse curiosity.

- Write clearly and lucidly using simple English, avoid slickness but use modern plain language, not the legalistic business phrases of yesteryear like 'I beg to inform...'

- Keep it brief! Select a number of selling points and concentrate on those — never go over one side of A4.

- Do not talk about 'we', going on about how good your business is and what you have done. Place emphasis on the benefits to the reader, talk about 'you'.

- Encourage action in the same way a good advertisement or salesman does — associate the letter with enclosed material and the reply procedure and demand action, now!

There are several ways in which a letter may be produced, but the more personalised it is, the higher the response. Never have the letter printed in printer's type — always use a typewritten format. The letter should look like a letter and as though it has been produced for each reader personally. Word processors have revolutionised the office and nowhere is this more apparent than in the reproduction of sales correspondence.

If the letter is the salesman, then any material enclosed should be regarded as sales aids. Material is most usually sales literature — brochures, leaflets, catalogues or price lists — but samples and free gifts may also be included. A reply card or easy-to-return order form should always be included when direct response is required, and it should not ask the respondent to do too much — two or three ticks and a signature at the most. Pre-paid postage return works to increase response from consumers but is less important for business respondents when its use is probably a waste of money.

It must always be remembered that sales correspondence has to compete for the recipient's attention with other mail, telephone calls, personal visits and day to day work. It must be attractive, to the point and as brief as possible, while being comprehensive enough to fully explain the product or service on offer. Do not be too optimistic about rates of response — the norm for a buying-decision response is 1% to 2% and for further-information response around 5%. Free gifts and attractive offers may increase the response and the quality of the list will also affect it. But it will be the quality of the package as a whole that has most impact and each element must be done in a professional way. Never send poor quality, badly written rubbish — it is a waste of time and money.

CORPORATE IMAGE

Branding is a technique used extensively by the large consumer companies. The principle is to establish a clear image for a particular product or product range and to put all marketing resources behind building and reinforcing that image. Industrial companies do the same but base their effort on promoting the company as a whole, rather than any individual product — oil companies, chemical giants, airlines, banks and many more can be observed in action every day of our lives.

All this effort is not undertaken for nothing — smaller businesses would do well to follow the example set by their larger colleagues, as the benefits to be gained from developing a sound corporate identity are considerable. Consistency and repetition generate a feeling of trust and the appearance of an established business that knows what it is doing, helps to foster good staff relations, provides better customers and lays the foundations for future expansion and diversification.

It is true to say that nowadays more businesses project a corporate image than a few years ago. But, sadly, there still are far too many (even some very large ones) that have failed to do so. The amazing thing about it is that it costs very little to do — material must still be produced — all it takes is a little thought and care. The business must start with a basic theme, and once established, all that is necessary is to stick rigidly to that theme in every contact ever made with the outside world.

- Establish a logo — a graphic design which may be based on the company name or an abstract design attached to the company name.

- Colour is very important, once the company's colours have been selected they should be used throughout printed material, display material, equipment and packaging.

- The theme of the company's image must reflect the type of business in which it operates and the basic approach it has to trading. If a firm is trading hard on prices in a competitive retail business it must have a bright and alert image — on the other hand, a business consultant should not appear too flashy.

- Logo, colour, design and style must run through every aspect of the firm's dealings — advertising, promotions, vehicles, shop and business signs, sales literature, stationery, packaging, uniforms, shop and exhibition display equipment and material, and, when possible, on the product itself.

It is consistency that counts. Whenever any item is produced it must be made perfectly clear to staff, agencies and
printers what the image is and what they must do to maintain it. This is not to say that the image is rigidly static, it
may change but only in a slow and steady evolutionary way
to reflect changes in fashion and trading patterns. It takes
time to establish a corporate identity but once there it
makes the launch of new products easier (customers already
know and trust the name) and helps the business as it grows
into new markets.

SPECIAL PROMOTIONS

Special promotions may be applied to consumers or trade
operations. They are normally designed to create rapid and
short-lived increases in business, although taken as a planned
campaign over a period of time, a series of promotions can
lead to permanent increases in trade. Promotions are often
used to assist in the launch of a new product or a change in
price, packaging or product range. As with all marketing
activity, special promotions must be part of an overall plan
and each campaign must be planned, controlled and monitored.

A promotion may stimulate new uses or new markets for
established products, it may be designed to attract bargain-
hunters or off-season sales, or to get competitors' customers
to try your product. Trade promotions may have the effect
of gaining shelf space for your product or create dealer
interest. Before embarking on a promotion, the smaller
business owner or manager must establish what is to be
achieved, as the range of techniques available is so large
that to get any idea of the best method to use, clear objectives must be set.

There are literally thousands of different types of promotions that have been used over the years, and the business owner or manager would do well to keep a constant
look out for ideas that may be appropriate for his product

or service. Many promotions are suitable for both consumer and trade efforts, and the most effective for any particular set of circumstances can only be found with a combination of common sense, testing and experience, but *always* starting from a written set of objectives and a clear idea of budget. As a guide, there follows a list of some of the more popular ideas.

- *Price-off pack* — a simple flash on the normal pack or a specially printed label offering money off that particular purchase — most often seen on fast-moving-consumer-goods, but also used for the trade on catering packs and on larger durable items on sale in retailers.

- *Premium offers* — again most often used with fmcg they offer goods at special prices usually in exchange for multiple proofs of purchase which are sent to the manufacturer. Alternatively, a premium offer may be attached to a product and either paid for at the counter (razors are a good example) or given free.

- *Bonus packs* — here the customer is given extra quantity for the same price, 20% more is a common sight in chemists and supermarket.

- *Buy one, get one free* — either attached to the product on the shelf or pack includes a voucher to be sent to the manufacturer.

- *Coupons* — delivered through the door, incorporated in an advertisement, available in-store or printed on the package (money-off next purchase), coupons are a very attractive way of obtaining a trial. Not just restricted to consumer goods, coupons are used extensively throughout business and may be used by smaller firms, especially on a local basis.

- *Free samples* — limited to certain products with low unit value and high repeat purchase. Very effective way of obtaining trial but is expensive in terms of the product given away and in terms of complex handling.

● *In-store demonstration* — often used in conjunction with free samples where it cuts down the handling problems, and where a complicated concept needs to be demonstrated. Also used when there is an element of 'unbelievable' novelty, where the skills of the market trader are in clear evidence.

● *Competitions and contests* — very effective for trade promotions where they may be used to gain shelf space or higher stocking; often carried out through salesmen. Consumer competitions are generally more difficult and have to be very attractive to gain sufficient interest.

● *Co-operative schemes* — between manufacturer and manufacturer or manufacturer and dealer, both contribute to offering a special deal to users which is mutually beneficial. Helps to keep the costs down and can be very effective in trade promotions.

● *Special discounts* — used in the trade to offer special discounts either on certain products or all products for a limited period. Useful to encourage the movement of slow lines and to sell out-of-season or finished lines.

● *Limited period quantity rate terms* — aimed at increasing stocking by offering generous quantity rate terms for a limited period. Often used when introducing a new product or expanding business to new geographical areas.

● *Clearance sale* — used commonly by retailers to dispose of out-of-season and finished lines. But a 'sale' may be used by the less scrupulous to move sub-standard or poor quality goods — although they now have to watch the law very closely. Clearance sales are also used by industrial sellers when they move premises or develop new products.

Once the business owner or manager has set objectives, determined his budget and selected the form of promotion to be used, the timing of the exercise must be worked out and a method of evaluating the results constructed. It is no good just firing off sales promotions without carefully planning them and monitoring the results. Even the large consumer companies can make mistakes — some have lost a vast amount of money because an offer was too attractive and it lasted too long. The choice is then either to disappoint customers or spend a great deal over budget to please them. Other promotions, of course, go off like a damp squid. Planning and testing will reduce the risks but the machinery for evaluation must be set up.

DISPLAY

Like special promotions, there are thousands of techniques with which a business may display itself and its products or services. The packaging itself is a form of display (this is covered in Chapter 12), material is used at exhibitions and trade fairs, at the point of sale, on sales staff and equipment and through all forms of communication. The basic principle is to follow the corporate image at all times, and to approach all display material with professionalism.

Retailers require effective point-of-sale material which they must sometimes provide for themselves. However, many manufacturers and importers produce point-of-sale material and the competition to get this into retail stores is immense. The smaller manufacturer will therefore have to produce good quality material if it is to stand any chance of success. Items must be relevant and not too ambitious — a six-foot by four-foot poster is not going to stand much chance of appearing in a retailer's window although a small well designed open/closed sign may. A flimsy display unit with sharp edges will soon find its way into the bin, but a compact item showing products in an effective way is likely to end up on the counter. Some research is necessary and it is worth asking salesmen regularly for their ideas.

A great deal of money is spent on T-shirts, diaries, pens, notepads, ashtrays and many other sundry display items. There is no doubt that much of this expenditure produces results; but a lot of it is wasted. Before jumping at the first idea that is placed in front of you, look around. Read the marketing press and decide exactly what the purpose of the promotional aid is to be, and what type would be most relevant to the recipients. Ask yourself: 'Would I want one of these if I was in that position?' If you wouldn't then you know not to lumber anyone else with that item; if you would, look around for a better idea. Only after thorough investigation and comprehensive searching should you go ahead with a promotional investment. After all, scarce resources should always be spent in the most productive and effective way.

SPONSORSHIP

Some of the most spectacular promotional deals in recent times have involved sponsorship, a promotional technique enjoying more and more support. Nobody had ever heard of Cornhill insurance until it clinched the best ever sponsorship deal with the cricketing world. The company has received unparalleled television and newspaper coverage at a cost each season less than some firms spend on one short television advertising campaign.

Again, the business owner or manager must be clear in his own mind as to what would be achieved if his company went into sponsorship. Once the objectives are clear an area of sponsorship must be found that meets objectives and fits in with the company's overall image and requirements. The main reasons for sponsorship are: to support other advertising and promotional effort; to boost the marketing profile of the business as a whole (e.g. local sports shop supporting local football league); or to support community public relations by showing that the company is socially responsible.

There are several opportunities in sponsorship for the smaller business, but owners and managers must apply the old test: 'Is there a better way of spending this money?' Frankly, the answer for the smaller firm is nearly always 'yes'. Nevertheless, sponsorship does sometimes pay off for the smaller business and often provides the owner with a way of being involved in something he or she is personally very interested in. What are the opportunities? Sport, cultural events, publications, exhibitions, education, charities, professional awards and local events all require support — many find it from company sponsorship. One warning: the initial cost is rarely the total cost of participation, sponsors will often have to supply display equipment, staff and further resources to cope with foreseeable and not so foreseeable contingencies.

EXHIBITIONS AND TRADE FAIRS

There is at least one, and sometimes many major exhibitions for almost every trade and profession. In addition, there are local and national general business and trade fairs and many overseas events. Essentially they are marketplaces where customers come to sellers and get the opportunity to inspect competitive suppliers at close range. It is for this very reason that exhibitors must take the utmost care in their stand preparation and presentation at the event itself. Under close scrutiny and in direct comparison, the company and its products or services have to look very good indeed. The golden rule is — if you can't do it properly, don't do it at all.

Exhibitions rarely pay for themselves in orders taken – they are generally a place to make new contacts, demonstrate new or complicated products and build goodwill. In the case of exporters, fairs and exhibitions are often the only places to make contacts and for this reason generous help is available from government through the British Overseas Trade Board and some Trade Associations.

Before attending an exhibition, business owners or managers must find out the types of visitors and the nature of the other stands likely to be there. Unless it is a new event (which must be treated with care) always visit the exhibition the year before you intend to show there. Organisers' literature can be very misleading and there are many firms that have exhibited at what appeared on the face of it to be an appropriate event, only to find that they stood out like a sore thumb and that there were no customers of any relevance to them.

Once the decision has been made, meticulous planning must be done – you can always spot the exhibitor that thought he could turn up with non-sales staff, a table and a couple of shelves five minutes before the doors open. Precise plans of the stand area, furniture required, lighting, display, literature, samples, demonstration models, electrical power, telephone, order processing, stand construction and dismantling, transport, accommodation, entertainment, audio-visual, staff rotas and press relations must be made. Customers and potential customers should be invited – it is no use only relying on passing trade. To cope with the immense planning burden, one member of staff must be made responsible, there will be a great deal of organising and paperwork to be done – this is not really the job for the happy amateur.

PRINTING AND PRINTED MATERIAL

There is absolutely no reason for a business ever to produce shoddy printed material. Every printed item is an ambassador for its source, either one that promotes it or does it down — and there is no excuse for a business that does itself down. Modern printing techniques mean that good quality printed material can be produced as cheaply and as fast as poor quality duplication, and when it comes to more complex jobs such as brochures and colour work it is false economy to cut corners. Remember the corporate identity and produce all printed material in line with the company's image.

It pays for every business owner and manager to understand the basics of printing. The most relevant system nowadays is small offset-litho, used by most local jobbing printers and the ubiquitous instant print firms. Essentially these machines will reproduce exactly what is presented in the form of artwork through a simple photographic process. This means that headlines can be produced with Letraset, pictures and photographs can be incorporated; copy may be reproduced from a good quality typewriter (for sales letters, etc) or from typesetting which these printers will do at reasonable cost. Colours may be used (spot colour) relatively cheaply although full-colour work is expensive and outside the scope of most instant print firms.

Price lists, catalogues, brochures, leaflets, stationery and visiting cards can be produced incorporating the corporate image, which should also be extended through order forms, invoices and all business paperwork. With a little care and attention all printed material can carry a sales message — not an obvious one, but a consistent and repetitive image of professionalism and trust. In these cases it costs no more to be effective — surely the best deal marketing has to offer?

BELOW THE LINE

CHECKLIST

1 Have you considered using mail order as an alternative to your present channels of distribution?
2 If you use mail order, or plan to, have you examined the three basic techniques to see which most suits your needs?
3 Have you considered the use of direct mail as a promotional tool and compared its cost with your existing promotions?
4 Do you maintain a mailing list of your customers from which it is simple to produce labels and easy to keep up to date?
5 Are you aware of directories and other publications that may contain sources of names and addresses of use to your business?
6 Can you name agencies from which you can rent lists of names and addresses likely to be of use to your business?
7 When you send a mailing of any sort, do you always enclose a sales letter?
8 Whenever you send a sales letter do you make it as personalised as is possible under the circumstances?
9 Are you aware of the basic rules that apply to writing effective sales letters?
10 Do you know what response rate you may expect from a mail shot?
11 Have you an established corporate image with logo, company colours and a house style?
12 Have you carefully assessed the benefits to be gained from using special promotions for your trade or public customers?
13 Are you aware of all the possible forms of special promotion?
14 Have you considered using display material to promote your business and is it in line with your corporate identity?
15 Are you wasting money on ineffective promotional aids?
16 Would sponsorship help you to meet your objectives?
17 Do you attend trade fairs or exhibitions and do you plan with meticulous care if you do?
18 Do you understand the principles of small offset-litho printing?
19 Have you ever produced shoddy material?

11
Public Relations

The Institute of Public Relations defines the practice of public relations as: 'the deliberate, planned and sustained effort to establish and maintain mutual understanding between an organisation and its public.' A business enterprise has several 'publics': customers, employees, investors, the community, and other businesses (suppliers and distributors). As an element in the marketing mix, public relations should be seen as promoting the interests of the company as a whole with the long term aim of improving business.

Good <u>internal</u> relations should be developed. Employees work more efficiently and loyally if they are treated well and kept informed of their employer's successes and developments. This relationship is just as important for shareholders and other investors who require confidence if they are to continue their support. Most large companies produce some form of newsletter, have regular meetings and arrange staff outings, Christmas parties, etc. Although smaller businesses may not have access to such large resources they would do well to follow the principles.

A business is a personality in its own right and will be judged on the image it presents to the outside world. <u>External</u> public relations effort must be directed towards developing this image; a bad reputation spreads like wildfire and there are plenty of consumer groups to make sure it does! Poor public relations go a long way towards destroying other marketing efforts; for example, no salesman should ever be placed in the embarrassing and wasteful position of having to apologise for his employer.

For the smaller business, contact with the press and broadcasting organisations is the most obvious way to improve its public profile. News items in the press, radio and television which mention a company's name, achievements or products can only be secured by a planned and continuous campaign. The occasional poorly presented press release, not followed up, is unlikely to bring any results. Feature articles on the company in the columns of local and trade publications may be arranged and do a great deal to increase awareness and arouse interest. Selecting the best media is tricky and must be approached thoughtfully — a national newspaper is not likely to be interested in a long, in-depth analysis of a technological development whereas a trade journal might.

Many businesses employ the services of a public relations consultant who brings an element of professionalism as well as established contacts. Unlike advertising agencies, PR consultants are paid a fee based on their time so it is important to link payment with performance. Results are judged on the amount of coverage (measured in column inches or centimetres or air time) achieved, although some coverage is clearly worth more than others in terms of impact.

Receptions and conferences for the press or the trade are excellent ways in which to generate goodwill and foster better public relations. Launching a new product, opening a new store or announcing a major change in marketing policy are events that provide a suitable focus of attention. But organisation is paramount: the venue, provision of refreshments, staffing, and display or demonstration material should create an atmosphere of calm efficiency; a disorganised meeting where the food and drinks run out hardly improves the image!

INTERNAL RELATIONS

Whatever the size of a business, a happy atmosphere at work and in the workplace is vital. The psychological need of every member of staff – worker or boss – to be wanted, understood and considered is often underestimated. Even the most junior member of staff is part of the team and must be made to feel an important cog in the wheel of business. Indeed, the most menial of jobs can often turn out to be the most valuable; after all, filing sounds, and often is, tremendously tedious, but quick and efficient document retrieval can spell the difference between making or losing a deal, or rescuing a transaction that is about to founder.

Although good internal relations is a matter for *all* managers, the means of systematically organising the way the business approaches this activity, and seeing that it is done properly, is the function of public relations. The day-to-day operation of the company will determine style – members of staff in a smaller business usually call each other by their first names – but rank must be established and evident when necessary. In certain fields, notably retailing, a hierarchy will be established and managers will be known as Sir, or Ms Smith.

It is important to ensure the internal 'feel' of the business reflects the external image it is trying to project, especially when the business is on permanent show to the public – retailing again. The whole effect of superb external relations – luxury glossy brochures and huge sums spent on advertising – may be lost if your staff are always complaining that the lavatory leaks, the premises are an eyesore or the workshop is in a disgusting mess.

Recruitment of the right staff is at the centre of this policy, but having recruited good staff they must want to stay, and they must feel content. If they don't they may lose you customers. Internal relations can deteriorate incredibly quickly, often through unrecognised and unrelated incidents; in other words, bad communications. *All* employees need to be kept informed about the business *they* work for. The grapevine is pervasive; if staff aren't told what is going on by you — be sure someone else will tell them. And it may not be accurate; there is nothing worse than finding groups of ill-informed people gossiping about the company's business.

People generally only produce their best when they are given active encouragement. Part of this has to be through financial incentive — bonus schemes, commission and over-time payments — but this is certainly not all that is needed. The majority of people respond to being made to feel that what they are doing is important, not only to the company but to themselves. True job satisfaction can only come in a 'caring business'; a hackneyed phrase yet one which has proved true over and over again.

In a very small business, there should be few difficulties in making sure that all staff know all they want about what they are doing, why and how it is valuable. As companies grow, however, various levels of communication can begin to establish themselves — and this is rarely beneficial. If managers concern themselves only with the theory of running the business while others discuss only the practicalities, a communication gap has been established. One way round this is to have regular informal discussion meetings, over coffee maybe, but make them brief — little and often is a useful adage.

If your business is enjoying a run of success — new export orders, record sales — tell the staff. If it's having a hard time — losing money, problems with planning — tell them that as well. Remember that, above all else, your staff *are* the company, and without them you would not be in business.

EXTERNAL RELATIONS

Marketing starts with the customer, and the way customers see a business as an organisation can make or break it. If the illusion is created that a business is a sprawling multinational when in reality it is only very small, customers can't help but be disappointed when they actually see it. And make no mistake, over a period of time many customers will see the business and the myth will be exploded – and the company out of business. The reality must match the image created for it.

Customers often have a preconceived idea of what they expect a business to be like; it may be useful to foster this. Take, for example, a small firm manufacturing chocolates. The general public will assume (probably because they have seen it on TV) that all the staff wear overalls, white hats and possibly surgical boots, and work in an almost hospital-like environment. They are of course quite right in this assumption; any food manufacturing has to be carried out in ultra-clean conditions by law. Making the most of this situation so that staff are seen with sparkling white overalls and all the gear, will reinforce people's attitudes towards the business.

If the same small company takes a little extra care, perhaps encouraging parties of visitors (women's groups, school parties) to see the goods being made and the ultra-clean conditions, it can do nothing but good. But a slipshod attitude towards the promotion and packaging and the odd second-rate soft centre and all the good will be undone. Public relations is putting across a complete package to the public at large and the customers in particular.

It can be said that the salesman is the sharp end of a company's marketing, and no salesman should ever be turned into an apologist for his employer – either for the quality of the product or any of the back-up he or she will expect from the company. The salesman must give out an aura of total belief in the product he is selling, with the faith in his company to meet his claims. But it works both ways, there is nothing worse than visiting a shop only to find that none of the sales staff *know* anything about the products they are dealing with. Customers, who are frequently experts themselves, lose patience and sales are lost.

External public relations must always reflect the truth; it is no help promoting an 'immediately available' image if there is a six weeks' waiting list. Once their interest is aroused only to be shattered by disappointment customers are unlikely to return later for repeat business. The general public are notoriously fickle and they will certainly not tolerate lies, even little white ones. Also, customers expect good after-sales service, and consumer legislation has given millions the means and confidence to stand up for their rights. An efficient money back or goods exchange service is a vital part of marketing activity when dealing with other businesses or the public — look at Marks and Spencers if you need proof.

But dealing with the public as customers is not the only arena for effective external public relations. Businesses should foster good relations with other businesses in the area, even those in a similar trade, the local community and local officials. Most important of all is the relationship with the media — local, trade and national — which provide a crucial link with all 'publics'. More about the press later in this chapter. Being involved with the local schools, sports teams, council, Round Table, Lions and Rotary are all aspects of good public relations, the usefulness of which should not be overlooked.

A surprising number of new customers are generated by word of mouth, personal recommendation or just customer to customer mention. This is further argument for good customer service and for as wide a spread of the message as possible. Establish the image you want for your business and ensure that any dealing you have with any member of the public is consistent with that image.

CONTACT WITH THE MEDIA

The power of the media should never be underestimated and certainly not ignored, but remember that it is not almighty. Local radio and newspapers are very approachable, as is the trade press. Each is a business in its own right and staffed with ordinary people. Make sure that you know all the local newspapers, local radio stations and relevant trade publications; foster a contact in each of the important ones and make sure that they know of you and what you do. Most journalists only know of particular businesses because they've been told about them.

All media is constantly looking for news, that is their job, so if you have any, tell them. Surprisingly, most businessmen never contact journalists, in the mistaken belief that they will not be interested in what they have to say. But once a particular journalist knows that you exist and have something interesting to say, he or she will come to you looking for news or comment on something else that is happening.

The chances are, that if you have something interesting to say, and you say it in the right way, the local newspaper or trade magazine will print it. Details of major orders, export triumphs, record business figures or an Award could well find its way into print and, importantly, put your company's name in front of the public. Even something unrelated to your business itself, like a member of staff winning a painting competition, can do the trick.

Don't be afraid of contacting the media, it will cost only the price of a telephone call (ask for the News Editor if you do not have a special contact) and a stamp if you send details. Although printed media is used most, do not forget local radio and television. With the advent of more and more truly local stations, news is a problem for them. There is a shortage of business people prepared to take a little time off to discuss affairs of interest. And the extensive use of phone-in programmes provides excellent opportunities to get your message across.

Many local radio stations maintain a panel register of people from all walks of life and all interests to provide back-up for general interest programmes and to sit at the other end of phone-in sessions. An aspect of business is often featured and, if you appear, you will be introduced by your own name *and* your company's name, its business and location. This again puts you in the public eye and you will be able to build up a reputation around your own personal image.

Many business owners and managers who have not dealt with the media tend to worry that journalists will report on items that will be damaging to their businesses. There is only one answer to that. If a journalist writes something adverse about your company then it is probably your own fault — you have created the wrong impression. With very few exceptions, most journalists are not in the business of damaging other people's business (they are the advertisers who keep the media going); this is particularly true of local and trade publications.

Nevertheless, relationships with members of the press are not always easy — your first meeting could be the last if you get it wrong. Maintain a friendly rapport, invite them to visit your premises and show them exactly what your company does, and how it does it. Give them small samples, but do not attempt to give journalists very expensive items, it will not help in any way, a throwaway ballpoint with your company's name printed on will do. And expensive lunches do not always impress (neither do bad ones), and remember that journalists are busy people and have deadlines to meet; do not waste their time.

Apart from the personal contact, if you have a piece of news that may be of general interest you should issue a press release and in certain circumstances hold a press conference. These methods are discussed in detail later in this chapter.

Remember too, that contact with the media may not

always be in happy circumstances. Journalists have good contacts, that is their job, and will know almost as soon as you do if you have been burgled, had a fire, or a serious accident has occurred on business premises. If a journalist should contact you, asking questions about an unfortunate incident, apart from accidents it may be the loss of a major contract or a salesman has run off with the sales manager's wife, be polite, answer questions courteously, be honest, and bear in mind the feelings of any third parties concerned. The expression 'no comment' only ever causes suspicion and in these cases nothing is ever 'off the record'.

THE PRESS RELEASE

The basic tool in external public relations for any organisation is the *Press Release*. For many smaller businesses, especially new ones, the only practical way of getting publicity is to issue press releases. If nothing else it will inform the journalists and editors of the existence of the business, its personalities and of course its telephone number and address.

A business may decide very early on to use a PR consultant, a choice that will be discussed later, or produce releases internally. If the latter course is taken, a person within the company — managing or marketing director is best — should take full responsibility to avoid embarrassing failures and conflicting stories. Department heads should never be allowed to issue their own press releases and any press enquiries should be directed to the one person responsible.

There are a few golden rules which, if followed, will increase the chances of success, i.e. get you into print. The first: 'Is this piece of information important or interesting enough to warrant a press release or will I be wasting my time and money?' Having decided that it is, the next step is presentation and composition. It is an unfortunate fact of life that press releases are notoriously awful — badly written, uninformative and, worst of all, tediously boring.

Editors everywhere complain about this and complaint is not just restricted to in-company releases, many 'professional' efforts are just as bad.

The dos and don'ts

Always: ● Use a bold identifying *heading* saying PRESS RELEASE or NEWS RELEASE, preferably printed in a colour or black on coloured paper

● Use the company *logo* in the company colours

● Stick to the same format and journalists will become familiar with your style

● Use a relevant and informative *title*, 'John Black joins Bloggs' or 'New range of silk purses'. It is from the title that the editor will decide whether or not to use the release

● Start with an interesting and succinct *opening* paragraph containing most of the details – company name, subject of the release and newsworthy highlights

● Follow up with two or three body paragraphs describing the advantages of the new product/ service, its applications, users and market at which it is aimed, *OR* short description of the person's new responsibilities and a brief career résumé, *OR* details of new order/export/award and a brief company profile *OR* details of the new marketing plan/shop/factory/lorry including how much it is going to cost

● Include *specifications and prices* in a short paragraph of around 40 words

Always:
(cont'd)

- *List at the end* of the release: name and telephone number of *contact* for further information, the *date* (very important) embargoed only in exceptional circumstances and the name, address and telephone number of the *company.*

- Use only *one side* of A4 paper for the main release

- Attach *further details* on separate sheets if needed, technical data, lists of suppliers, etc

- Attach a reasonably-sized, good quality black and white *photograph* that is interesting and well captioned

- Use good straightforward *English* matching the style of the publications at which the news is aimed

- *Follow-up* with telephone calls to those media considered most important and most likely to use the information

But, just as important as what you should do is what you should not.

Never:

- Use superlatives

- Use unsupportable claims such as 'unique', 'revolutionary'

- Incorporate 'puff' — self-praise

- Make claims which are clearly suspect; 'the world's cheapest', 'the only . . .'

- Use vague generalisations such as 'economical' — say why it is, or 'efficient' — explain its performance

Never: ● Drift into mid-Atlantic jargon; 'on-going situa-
(cont'd)   tion', 'consumer utilisation' etc

       ● Tell lies (!)

       ● Clutter the heading with company address, etc.

An example of a well presented press release (which accompanied a black and white photograph) is shown in Fig 11.1. But it should be remembered that, if at all possible it is better to tailor-make a press release to suit the medium to which it is sent. For example, a technical journal will want more detailed information written to its' technically-minded readers, but the *Sun* newspaper will certainly not.

Although the majority of business press releases are concerned with new products or services, personnel, developments, etc, the less serious 'newsy' press release can also meet with success. Perhaps the company football or darts team has won the league, or staff have collected money for charity in an unusual way. These opportunities should not be overlooked, and the visit of a VIP is always worth a few column inches.

Unfortunately, as we have seen above, news is not always good. Press releases can be a useful way of clearing the air or setting the record straight, or providing customer information in the sad event of a major fire where alternative arrangements for the supply of goods have to be made. Releases may also be issued if a company is going out of business or where a well-known and respected member of staff dies.

Where to send them

Having written and produced our press release, no matter how superb it may be, it is of little use until it is in the right hands. A mailing list of all relevant media should be established and maintained, updating with the appearance of new

NEWS RELEASE

Date of Issue: 13.1.82
FOR IMMEDIATE RELEASE

UK SPECIALIST CRACKS FAR EAST PLASTIC COMPONENTS MARKET

A specialist plastic mouldings and diecasting company in Alcester, Warks, has won a major contract to supply 8 million plastic bobbins to a Taiwannese manufacturer of tape cassette players. Dynacast International Ltd is to supply 4 million each of two types of bobbins for use in the record/play-back head assemblies of the cassette players. The bobbins are to be manufactured in 30% glass filled nylon using a technique developed by Dynacast.

Dynacast's unique moulding system enables extremely fine tolerances to be achieved without the need for any finishing operations.

Steve Bullen, Dynacast's Marketing Manager, explained: "This contact was won not only on our price competitiveness but also on the extremely high quality of the finished product we can offer. With tolerances as low as 20 microns, the bobbins require exactly the type of precision moulding that we can provide."

Before coming to Britain for these particular components the company was having the bobbins made in Taiwan. "The company was experiencing considerable problems with a large number of bobbins being rejected at the quality control stage," continued Mr Bullen. "Having proved that we could provide the components at a highly competitive price we had to show that we were capable of not only reaching the required technical specification but also of maintaining that standard. Once that had been proved the contract was in the bag!"

ENDS

INFORMATION CHECK: James Blackledge
DAY TEL NO: 021-550 1827   NIGHT TEL NO: Tewkesbury 294130

Dynacast International Ltd
Arden Forest Industrial Estate
Tything Road, Alcester
Warks B49 6EW   Telephone: 0789 763322 Telex: 311447

Issued on behalf of DYNACAST INTERNATIONAL Ltd. Arden Forest Industrial Estate, Alcester, Warwickshire B49 6EW.
by Nicholas Mendes & Associates Limited ☐ registered public relations consultants
Midland House, New Road, Halesowen, West Midlands, B63 3HY ☐ 021-550 1827 & 1828 ☐ Telex 337439

Fig. 11.1. An example of a well presented press release . . .

publications and the disappearance of others. Releases should be sent to news editors or other editors and journalists *by name* whenever possible, if not, addressed to the 'News Editor' and marked 'Press Material'. Whether first or second class post is used is a matter of personal preference and urgency.

It is well worth discovering the copy deadlines by which material has to reach a publication, particularly in the case of weekly and monthly magazines and newspapers. If you just miss a monthly's deadline your news could be three months out of date by the time it is printed, and will more than likely get 'filed in the bin'.

PUBLIC RELATIONS CONSULTANTS

Businesses usually switch from do-it-yourself public relations to employing a PR consultant for one of two reasons: they have become so large or successful that the amount of time taken up by a key executive in carrying out the activity is excessive; or because the business requires a professional approach to public relations as part of its marketing plan. But there is no doubt that using a consultant can reap rewards far greater than the cost.

Unlike advertising agencies, PR consultants obtain their income wholly from the fees they charge based on how much time they spend working for their clients. In its simplest form, a consultant will just consult – advising on how the company may best approach the activity. But this is unusual; more often the consultant is appointed to provide an all-up service, from writing and issuing press releases to arranging royal visits, and everything in between.

The decision of whether or not to use a consultant should depend on a number of things, not the least important of which is money. Although it may appear to be an expensive service, the use of a PR consultant can actually save money – in management time which would be better spent on other company activities, and in long-term increased sales.

The geographical placing of a consultant is fairly important and, although there is a tendency to go for the big
London agencies, on balance it is probably better to use
one situated close to the company's main premises. Frequent
meetings will be necessary and you will be paying for travelling expenses. The consultant will expect, and should
be given, fairly free access to the business premises, and
staff should be made aware of who he or she is, and his
or her name. Any consultant worth his fee will spend time
in your premises getting to know how it all works.

PR consultants tend to specialise and if you have a specialist product or service employ one that knows your field.
After all, once appointed, the consultant will be acting on
your behalf — dealing with questions from the media, issuing
press releases and arranging visits. You must ensure that the
consultant's view of your business coincides with the one
you are trying to project (the consultant should be able to
help you decide on that), that his facts are right and that
you trust his or her judgment. A consultant can add a fresh
viewpoint to an otherwise inward-looking business and will
often see opportunities that the management has missed.

Businesses that have never had any dealings with PR
consultants will first need to acquaint themselves with
what is available once the decision to go outside for help
has been taken. The relevant listings in *Hollis Press and
Public Relations Annual* or similar directory will help, or
go to the Institute of Public Relations and ask for their
list. Contact a number of likely agencies and ask them all
to provide propositions should they win your account.
Choose whichever suits your purse and purpose best.

Reputable PR consultants and agencies will not normally
take on a client who is likely to be a direct competitor to
an account they already hold, because of possible conflict
of interests. For this reason you may not be acceptable
to a particular consultant, but you must try to find one

with knowledge of your field.

At initial meetings with the consultant it must be decided how much, or how little, work will be done on your behalf, how much you are prepared to spend (or what you will be charged) and what your objectives are — increased sales, higher public profile, creation of a new company image or increased consumer awareness. Ensure that you provide strict terms of reference to the consultant and that he knows he must not step outside them.

Your consultant should have at his disposal a number of facilities including the speedy and efficient typing, production and printing of press releases, comprehensive and current mailing lists, good photographers and established contacts in the media. Consultants will be able to write authoritative feature articles, arrange press conferences and receptions, design good brochures and help with the production of training and selling films and audio-visuals.

If you are a small and unknown company, it may well be worth appointing a large and established PR agency. It will have its own style and reputation and its work will be known to journalists and editors in the field. It may be useful to exploit this reputation and 'ride on their backs'. Press releases may come on their house paper and journalists are quick to spot new additions to a PR consultant's client list and will want to know more.

PRESS CONFERENCES AND RECEPTIONS

A badly run press event does more harm than good but if staged well can bring great reward. They must be run with precision — well planned, well organised and perfectly executed. If a PR consultant has been appointed he or she will handle the details, but it is such an important occasion the marketing director or managing director must be personally involved. A press event must be based on an important happening, where a press release is just not enough, and will bring in far more coverage if it is right.

- Once you have decided to hold a press event appoint someone to co-ordinate the whole thing. Someone has to be able to make final arrangements and know what the budget is.

- Plan the event well in advance bearing in mind the optimum date for the news and minimising coverage lost because of copy deadlines.

- Choose a suitable venue and *visit it yourself* to check it out and make sure that it is convenient for as many people as possible – hotels are often used. Book well in advance wherever you choose and have it confirmed *in writing*. Double check a few days before the event and finalise the numbers.

- Send out invitations in good time giving as many details as possible: nature of event, subject, venue, timetable, food and drinks. Ensure you ask for a reply.

- Provide a reception desk where guests can sign in (so you know who has come) and be directed to an organiser.

- Provide *everyone* with a lapel badge, remember lady journalists have no top pockets, adhesive labels are acceptable provided they do not contain any 'super-glue'. All badges should have names and titles/publications clearly marked.

- Ensure each journalist has adequate information (press-kit) in an easy-to-carry folder. The kit should contain a release, black and white photographs, background information and examples. Remember that the kit will be sent to journalists that could not attend, give full specifications, prices and charges.

● Make sure that journalists are not ignored and that there are sufficient members of staff in attendance.

● Refreshments should be of good quality, food is more important than drink and if alcohol is to be served there must be solid food and non-alcoholic alternatives.

● Stick to the timetable and do not go on for too long.

● Make sure working demonstrations *work* (!), feeble excuses like blown fuses will not wash, this includes slide shows.

● Speakers must leave time for questions and encourage them.

● Thank everyone for coming at the end of the event.

● Monitor the results by checking those publications that were represented.

PUBLIC RELATIONS

CHECKLIST

1 Do you make a planned and systematic effort to foster good internal and external public relations?
2 Do you arrange occasional social events for your staff?
3 Do you hold regular informal meetings to allow managers and staff to get together?
4 Have you a firm idea of what image your business should project?
5 Can you list all your local newspapers, local radio stations and relevant trade publications?
6 Have you contacts in all the above media and do you speak to them from time to time?
7 Have you designed a special form of notepaper for press releases?
8 Do you send press releases to the relevant media whenever you have any news?
9 Do you always limit the length of your press releases to one side of A4 paper and attach extra information and a black and white photograph?
10 Do you maintain an up-to-date media mailing list?
11 Have you carefully considered the benefits of using a PR consultant?
12 Have you a written plan to follow when you organise a press event?
13 Do you regularly invite journalists to visit your premises?

PART V
Product
Policy

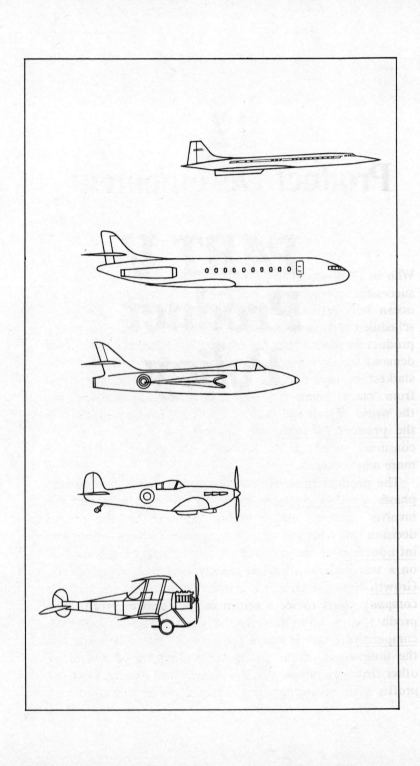

12
Product Development

Who in 1930 would have guessed that, despite many years of successful operation, by the 1980s there would not be one ocean liner regularly transporting passengers on year-round scheduled services between the United States and Europe. No product or service lasts for ever, either in terms of consumer demand or as a profitable part of a firm's business. The starkest examples of the limited appeal of products come from 'craze' items: the Yo-Yo, hula-hoop, skateboard, and the world of pop and fashion. This phenomenon is known as the product life-cycle and its major consequence in our consumer society is the relentless appearance of more and more new products.

The product life-cycle may be seen to have five distinct phases: development is undoubtedly the most important and involves research and planning followed by the crucial decision of whether or not to proceed. Next comes the introduction of the product on to the market; this may be on a test basis in a limited geographical area, or nationally. Growth comes next, and it is only during this phase that the company starts to see a return in the form of profits. The product now goes through the most difficult stage; the competitive phase is where good profits are to be made but the uniqueness of the product has disappeared and many other firms are jumping on the bandwagon. Finally, sales and profits start to decline and while some revitalisation may temporarily boost the useful life of some products, the inevitable decision must be made as to when to drop the product altogether.

The unavoidable nature of the product life-cycle gives new product development a particular significance to manufacturers of consumer goods although new products are just as vital for the success of all businesses. A 'new product' is one that is obviously different in the eyes of the customer — technical innovation plays a major role by producing entirely new products: computers, felt-tip pens, Concorde, fish fingers, and colour television are familiar examples. But a new product need not be something completely different: a new flavour toothpaste, blue specks in the washing powder, a different engine size in an existing motor car (or just a new trim), a new name and package, may be enough to provide a different image and a whole new market.

Launching a new product is a risky undertaking. Even after extensive research and competent planning new products have failed abysmally, and for the smaller business that means disaster. Some form of test market is the best way to reduce risks and the only way to provide evidence (as opposed to an indication) of likely success or failure. Test marketing must be well planned and executed and designed to provide maximum information by testing the right things, using a truly representative area, and carefully monitoring the results.

However, the intrinsic quality of the product or service itself is not the only consideration; packaging is also important and in some cases, more important. Packaging first and foremost must offer protection, but this is by no means all. It must provide convenience for storage and handling, and dsitinguish the product it contains from its competitors. Many packages serve to promote the product and to gain display in retailers; Tic-Tac Mints are an excellent example of how revolutionary packaging demands display space in an intensely competitive location.

PRODUCTS

In marketing terms a product is anything that a business offers to a market. It does not have to be a tangible thing, services such as travel agency, insurance and house repairs also display the characteristics of products. But it goes further than that; businesses offer a 'package deal' in every transaction — the actual product or service plus other elements such as advice, packaging, delivery, after-sales care and guarantees.

Although this chapter appears towards the end of the book product policy in terms of the 'package deal' offered by firms is the most central aspect of a business's marketing policy — the whole reason for being in business is to offer products to customers (and sell them). The business owner or manager must define the type, range and quantity of products offered, the 'package' his firm will be presenting, and when and how these products will be offered to the market. These major policy decisions will in turn affect the entire operation of the company, its position in the marketplace and how it approaches the market.

Businesses very rarely deal with just one product at a single price; they more usually offer a number of different items in a range of sizes and trims, and at differing prices depending on quantity and the associated 'package'. This collection is known as the product mix, which should be designed to smooth out the vagaries of seasonal trends and people's changing tastes, and maximise the use of resources. The advantages of a balanced product mix must be carefully weighed against the disadvantages of spreading one's efforts too thinly, and losing the economies of scale.

As the business owner or manager develops his marketing objectives, he will work from his product base. Different products need to be marketed in different ways and, although the distinction is often superficial, it is useful to distinguish between the different classes of products. The most obvious difference is between consumer, those products which will be offered direct to the end-consumer in their existing forms, and industrial products which are sold to other businesses. Companies that sell consumer products to intermediaries will need to combine industrial marketing skills with a knowledge of consumer end-users and, often, a marketing effort directed towards those consumers. Another useful distinction is between consumables, those products which are used up quickly (food, nuts and bolts, stationery, etc), and durables, products which last a relatively long time (cars, typewriters, washing machines, furniture, etc).

We have seen in previous chapters how these distinctions determine whether emphasis is placed on direct or indirect selling, but the nature of the product will also influence the firm's entire approach to marketing and the profile adopted by the business in the marketplace. But every business requires planned and co-ordinated marketing. There is a tendency for industrial companies in Britain to take the attitude that marketing is only for the consumer product companies. This is rubbish! And it is the main reason why British industrial firms have been consistently out-performed by Japanese, American and European competitors. All firms need *effective marketing* – different products merely dictate the emphasis the business will place on each element.

Sometimes these arbitrary distinctions may be misleading – specialist consumer consumables, such as exotic foods, can take on the characteristics of durables (especially if they are expensive) in that buying decisions are much more carefully considered and customers will go to great lengths to seek out exactly what they want. This is normally true of durable items; consumables are usually purchased in a less-considered way and convenience counts for much more than product identification.

Confusion may also occur with products that are bought by both consumers and industrial buyers. Certain stationery items, furniture, catering foods and hand tools are examples of items that can be classified as both industrial and consumer products. These items will require different marketing — hence the coexistence of builders' merchants and do-it-yourself shops, and trade counters in garages. Many larger companies get round the problem by setting up an industrial division, or even a separate company within a group — the smaller business will often have to make the best of an integrated operation.

The important thing is to recognise that there are different needs and to direct part of the marketing effort towards the alternative market. If the alternative market is small and less profitable, it is better to focus all attention on the main market in order to prevent effort being diluted and resources wasted on smaller and less cost-effective operations.

PRODUCT PLANNING

In addition to its tactical marketing effort, every business will have strategic considerations based on two elements — products and markets. At every stage of development, the business owner will have product/market decisions based on whether to look towards markets or products for development opportunities. Before making a decision as to which strategy to adopt, the business owner or manager will need to consider all alternatives carefully, deciding which product/market strategy most fits his needs.

Using existing products — Improved profitability may be gained by simplifications in the disign of existing products (less components or assembly operations), improved buying, or by streamlining marketing and production methods. A more aggressive marketing policy may increase market penetration; achieved through reinforced branding, harder direct or indirect selling, better merchandising or packaging changes. New markets may be found through establishing new uses and users for products or by widening geographical coverage at home or overseas.

Changing products — Sales may be improved by introducing changes to éxisting products. These changes may be in the form of new colours, sizes, designs or improved trim (car manufacturers are masters of developing existing products to stimulate sales). Alternatively a product range may be rationalised by removing less successful or obsolete products to allow more effort to be placed on improving markets for the remainder. A company may trade-up by offering a more expensive version of the product or trade-down by offering a cheaper one.

Introducing new products — A business may decide that the only way forward is to introduce new products. These may replace old products and be offered to existing markets through the existing marketing network. New products forming an extension to the range, or related to it in some other way, may be offered through planned diversification with the consequence of improving the company's place in the market. A business may go in for total diversification by introducing completely new products to new markets, a highly risky step to be taken only when all alternative strategies have been exhausted or potential profits are extremely high.

PRODUCT LIFE-CYCLE

The reason for all this constant attention to product development is the need for companies to maintain profits and their competitive positions in a marketplace where demand for products is always changing. Demand changes because of a number of factors: fashions, tastes, technological advances and changes in disposable incomes. All these factors add together in a most complex way with the end result that some products come and go at the most alarming rate. Some last only a matter of a few weeks, others for decades, but they all have a fixed period when they are in demand after which they die — a phenomenon known as the product life-cycle.

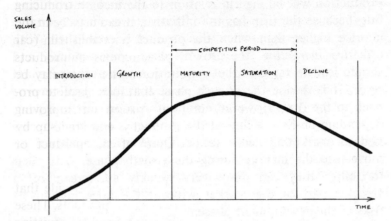

Fig. 12.1. The product life-cycle

The pattern of the life-cycle is not exactly the same for all products; some have a much steeper growth phase or a more rapid decline, and those with long lives reach a peak after which the curve flattens out in a plateau for a period of several years. The basic phases are, however, the same for all products and by studying market trends and figures the business owner or manager may establish about where each of his products stands in its life-cycle. Profits are highest in the early stages when competition is at a minimum and innovators may sell the product at a premium.

Before reaching the introduction phase, all new products undergo a difficult period of development and investment. This is when the innovating business is most vulnerable — new ideas require intense examination and screening to minimise the risk of expensive failure. Smaller businesses have a good reputation for innovation and their greatest advantage is the speed at which they can respond to the demands of the market — but only if they understand the market.

During the introduction fixed costs of marketing and

production will be high in relation to the income from sales but, because the firm has the initiative, it can usually charge a price higher than when the product is established. With *effective marketing*, the growth phase comes quickly and should lead to rapid market penetration even at the premium price. It is during the growth phase that most profits come back to the firm. However, competitors soon start to appear, depending on how technical the product is and how specialised its marketing needs to be. Quite often, smaller firms move into the market during the growth phase. With their flexibility they can move very quickly and cream off a valuable part of the market without the huge investment risks of the development phase.

Now comes the most difficult time for all in the market – the competitive period – when the maximum number of competitors are in the market and the prices are forced down. The first part of this period is the maturity phase as sales volume continues to rise, mainly due to greater exposure through a growing number of participating firms. This is still a time of opportunity and, although profit margins are lower, *effective marketing* should allow very reasonable returns for most competitors. During the saturation phase, which may be a long-term period of steady high volume sales, aggressive marketing is the only way to win a higher share of the total market.

As the product declines companies retract, concentrating on increased efficiency and attracting sales through aggressive pricing policy. Profits are much smaller and companies need to reassess their investment policies, looking towards investing in newer and more profitable product lines. Sentiment and hopes for revival often mask the objective requirement to drop an obsolete product, especially if it was part of the original product mix of the company.

New markets may be sought in less developed countries, especially if production investment is high (the process industries provide examples of companies constantly moving down-market on an international basis). Natural product obsolescence is a fact of life but, although these products can consume an inordinate amount of management time and other resources, companies are often slow to react.

NEW PRODUCT DEVELOPMENT

Despite the vast sums large companies spend on research and development, many of their new products fail shortly after being introduced to the market. Probably the most common cause of small business failure, apart from lack of management skills, is that their products are just not up to the mark. Altogether, some estimates put the rate of new product failure, across the board, as high as 80%-plus; but whatever the figure, one thing is certain – new product development is a very risky business.

Research and planning are critical during the time when ideas are formulated and as the business develops its ideas. Risk is highest when investment is at a peak, so all possible steps must be taken to eliminate products that will lead to failure *before* major investment has begun. Extensive planning is a must and a co-ordinated timetable of investment has to be established – engineering, plant, commercial back-up, personnel, financial and marketing resources will have to be scheduled. All these investments will be made before any return is possible and the risk grows and grows; before the product is launched and just after.

New product ideas come from many sources and the business owner or manager should be on constant alert. Ideas may be generated from inside the firm, from production and sales staff, from *ad hoc* research, customers, inspiration or as a result of planned and systematic investigation. Wherever the idea comes from, the first step is to examine the potential market for the new product and determine roughly what customers are likely to want. From this, a set of initial specifications can be created on which the business owner or manager can base further research and planning. If these specifications indicate that the new product will be outside the firm's general objectives, or will require resources that are not likely to be made available, the idea should be dropped immediately. This is no time for compromise (there are plenty of ideas) — at this stage investment will have been small, possibly only some of the owner's time, and it is true to say that *most* new product ideas should go no further than this stage.

If the new product idea does fit in with the company's objectives and available resources, the next step is to look more closely at the product, its market and the competition. Examine the market very carefully, gauge the likely sales, scale of the life-cycle and pattern of demand. Will the product show rapid growth or will it face a long hard haul? Is the idea easy to copy? Can you protect your idea with patents, copyright or trade marks? Is it a fad idea and, if so, how long will it last? Establish *exactly* what resources will be necessary and precisely how you plan to finance the project. If, at this stage, you discover that resources are going to be too much to handle, or that there is a flaw in the market, drop the idea and continue the search for a new one.

Have a good look at the competition or those firms most likely to respond to your initiative. Are other firms going to be in a better position than you to respond to demand? Competitors may already have the plant and equipment, available staff or a better marketing network. The chances of successfully launching a new product depend, to a great extent, on the lead you are able to generate over competitors; if you are unlikely to have much of a lead, think very carefully before proceeding with the idea. It is also worth examining ways of creating a lead by establishing a uniqueness in your product which will be heavily supported by its initial marketing.

This whole screening procedure should be meticulously followed for *every* new product before any major investment is made. Only after an idea passes through the screening process and adequate plans have been made should investment begin. But at all stages of investment the project must be carefully monitored and, if serious doubts arise as to potential markets and availability of resources, abandoned. Many smaller businesses go bust because they have not abandoned a loser, even after it has been recognised as such, merely on the basis of reluctance to waste investment part way through a project. It is better to waste some resources by pulling out of a failing project than risk the whole enterprise by carrying on regardless.

TEST MARKETING

Even after thorough screening and the successful implementation of an investment programme, the biggest test has yet to come (this is also usually the biggest single investment); introducing the product to the market. Often the smaller business, by necessity, will test the market and, after a successful start, move on to wider and wider market penetration. But, whatever the circumstances, it is wise to adopt the principle of test marketing for every new product. A marketing budget can increase alarmingly in the period immediately after the launch of a new product and, despite the risk of alerting competition, taking it steadily will help keep investment under control.

A controlled test market is normally based on a defined geographical area, although a cross-section of customers can work equally well. The large consumer companies invariably use a small television area (Anglia and Tyne-Tees are favourites) even if television advertising is not a major part of the campaign. The reason for this is that accurate statistical information is readily available and quantifiable for these areas. This makes monitoring and control more realistic, through having a sound information base on which to base results.

The important thing for any test market is to get as representative a test as possible. The test market is the first time that the business owner or manager will get real information as to how the market responds to the new product; up to this stage all the feed-back will be subjectively based. Care must be taken to avoid untypical influences, such as very densely or very sparsely populated areas; there should be a good cross-section of potential customers and you should not engage in any marketing activities that would not be repeated on a wider basis.

During the test market, constant reference should be made to the accounting criteria, such as break-even and margins, to ensure that the project is on line and is likely to prove viable. If results indicate that income from the product, in terms of sales and prices, is not likely to meet necessary targets, the project must be abandoned. Attempts at 'cutting losses' by 'going national' after a failed test market will lead to even greater losses in the end.

PACKAGING

To the marketer, a package is much more than a box, bottle, can, bag or carton. It is a medium through which he can promote his product, create a brand or corporate identity, gain display space in retailers and other intermediaries, demand attention, differentiate his product from others which are very similar, and make his product more saleable. Packaging is a vital element in the consumer marketing mix and is becoming more and more important to industrial marketing, as handling and office technology gets more sophisticated.

Recent developments in packaging materials have widened the options and have made packaging decisions among the most important in business life. There is, however, an unavoidable conflict of interest between the cost factor, demanding minimum expenditure for protection of products, and the marketing factors which demand more expenditure to achieve objectives. The smaller business owner or manager is likely to face this conflict in his own mind and will need to consider a number of factors before reaching a compromise.

Minimum requirements

First and foremost a package must afford protection to the product it contains, and this means at every stage of the distribution process. Warehouses, intermediaries and end-users will need to store and handle the product which may require protection against damage, contamination, evaporation, insect attack and theft. Packaging must also offer convenience in handling, storage and use, and thought must be given to where and how products are stored, outer protection and inner packages, and what form of transport is used to move the products. Consideration will also be given to reducing the cost factor in terms of transport.

Many products stay with their packaging when actually in use; foodstuffs are often dispensed direct from the pack, notepaper is kept in the box, instruments live in their cases and sprays come from aerosols. Care must be taken to cater for these needs and to facilitate easy use. Many products lose sales, not because of poor quality, but because their competitors offer more convenient packaging. Some packs are designed for re-use and, apart from offering convenience, act as a permanent reminder of the product.

Marketing requirements

A brief look around the men's cosmetics counter of any chemist or department store will show what can be achieved with packaging. Some after-shave lotions are country, others are city, some are green, some brown, some blue, some are for sailors and others are for martial arts experts. The liquids inside are very similar but the packaging establishes clear product differences which are supported by other promotional efforts. The packaging is so important to the cosmetics industry that quite often it costs more than the product inside.

Apart from establishing product differences, packaging can create images — brand or corporate. Branding is used extensively in fast-moving consumer goods marketing, but smaller businesses in all types of trade can promote an identity for themselves and their products through careful and effective packaging design. A package can also create an image of quality, uniqueness, good value or reliability. It is a very powerful marketing tool and the tendency towards self-selection in retail, wholesale and industrial suppliers has focussed a great deal of attention on it.

PRODUCT DEVELOPMENT
CHECKLIST

1 Can you identify all the elements of the 'package deal' you offer around each of your products?

2 Into which category does each of your products fit and do you place emphasis on the most relevant marketing activities.

3 Do you divide your marketing effort, if appropriate, into industrial and consumer operations?

4 Have you a strategic product/market policy and do you make a positive effort to follow this policy?

5 Are you aware of which stage in the life-cycle each of your products has reached?

6 Are you continuously searching for new product ideas and do you encourage your staff and customers to make suggestions?

7 Do you put all new product ideas through a thorough screening process before undertaking any investment?

8 When launching a new product, do you start with a well-planned and representative test market?

9 Does your packaging offer the best protection to your product at all stages of distribution and final use?

10 How are your products handled by users and distributors and could your packaging offer them more convenience?

11 Are you aware of the promotional value of packaging and do you make the most of the opportunities offered?

13
Pricing

In law, the title to goods passes only when consideration is made for those goods — for business this consideration is the price. According to economic theory, price is determined by the level at which supply meets demand and in terms of perfect competition this definition has some relevance. A street market is the nearest thing to perfect competition — each week we see how the forces of supply and demand battle out until the price is set for cabbages, oranges, pineapples and avocado pears.

But for most businesses, markets are distorted by complex economic pressures; price setting becomes a problem of policy. It is the elasticity of demand that is important; i.e., how fast sales decline with a given change in price. A small firm manufacturing simple components for other manufacturers is likely to see its sales disappear completely if it increases its prices above those of its competitors, a restaurant has greater flexibility.

Demand depends on the nature of the market, the position of the company within that market, the characteristics of the product and the strength of direct and indirect competition.

What the market will bear is a sound method of judging price but the complexity of establishing this level makes the use of the technique difficult. Many small firms find themselves in a market where the price is firmly set by a dominant leader, or by the trade in general. Others will have to set a price using available information – asking customers through controlled research will provide an indication of what people are prepared to pay, but as with all attitude research, the results may be misleading. Another method is to experiment by setting a minimum price, increasing it until there is an unacceptable reduction in sales and profit contribution.

Most firms however, will find that pricing policy is not just dependent on market forces. Businesses have to base their decisions on internal considerations and on profitability. The correct price is that which brings in maximum total contribution to profit; not necessarily the one that means most volume sales, and rarely the highest. This policy of cost-plus (in its simplest form) adds a pre-set margin to the purchase price of the item in question. This method is most usually employed by retailers and wholesalers where fixed costs are relatively static.

Manufacturers and firms in the service sector find that the biggest problem comes with determining the costs. Usual practice is to take production and material costs and look towards the 'margin' to provide a contribution to overheads and profit. Each item sold will make a contribution, and the business must plan to meet overheads and profit targets within a specified period of time through forecasting total sales. This method is particularly useful when dealing with a range of products or services; each one can be monitored to see if it is pulling its weight and providing an adequate contribution.

In practical terms, most smaller businesses will base pricing policy on a combination of 'what the market will bear' and 'cost-plus'. The emphasis will depend on objectives: whether the business owner decides to skim the market by picking off the most attractive prospects where price may be set solely on what the market will bear, or whether the business seeks to penetrate the market, capturing a significant part of it (even if only in a limited geographical area); here price will be cut right back and much more attention paid to costs and marginal profits.

Generally, a business will establish a minimum price based on costs, contribution to overheads, and profits, below which it is not worth operating. Owners and managers must find out how much customers will benefit from using their products or services and establish how much they would be willing to pay. Studying the competition is useful, but it is important to account for even the slightest product differences. Some experimentation is necessary, and businesses must beware of under-pricing, which inevitably leads to losses and subsequent failure.

DEMAND AND COMPETITION

Although it is true that price is closely related to supply and demand, individual firms have little control over either factor in terms of the market as a whole. Some large companies can influence demand in their sector of the market by aggressive marketing, but our highly competitive economy generally ensures that profitable monopoly is very short-lived. Smaller companies have even less influence than large ones and the key to effective pricing policy is for the owner or manager to have a good understanding of the factors that influence prices.

When economists talk about supply they are referring to total market supply and, in most cases, ignore any indirect competitive elements. In theory, it is therefore simple to come to a price level that fits this uncomplicated view of the market. Unfortunately for the theorists, a free economy ensures that a shortfall of supply of any profitable product line is soon made up. Because of this, the size of the market, varying levels of disposable income and complex competitive pressures, the effect of supply on pricing policy is so remote that it can, on the whole, be ignored by most businesses. The exception is in the world of commodities (basic foods, oil, etc.), where the market sets the prices and every business follows.

The business owner or manager should be much more concerned about demand, what influences it and what pattern it follows. Knowing the size of the total market will help and, although individual firms can do little about the whole, they must use price to influence their part of the market. But there are other influences that can greatly distort the demand for any individual product. These may best be illustrated by taking a simple example – a five-pound bag of potatoes.

At one time, when the economy was much simpler, the potato was an essential commodity and price was determined solely by reference to the marketplace. Nowadays, people are not starving – they can take or leave potatoes and clearly price will affect demand. But consumers may wish to buy a certain variety of potato (King Edward, for example), they may want to buy them loose from the greengrocer, or in a half-hundredweight sack from the farm shop. In Poland consumers buy what they can get their hands on – here, disposable incomes and mobility mean that consumers have a wide freedom of choice.

But the picture is far from complete. The demand for potatoes may be declining because fish and chip shops are disappearing. On the other hand, there is a growth in demand for filled baked potatoes. These harmless and nutritious vegetables have been accused of committing the modern world's deadliest sin – they are said to be fattening. Changes in tastes and fashions can greatly influence the demand for a product and the business owner or manager must be very much aware of current trends – they have a significant effect on demand and, consequently, price.

Competition comes directly from other types of potato and from other suppliers of potatoes on the grounds of price, quality and marketing. But it comes also from other quarters. Alternative vegetables may be used by the consumer as a replacement for potatoes, but a much bigger threat has come recently from other foods such as rice and pasta products. Pricing policy needs to account for direct and substitute competitors — if there is a price benefit for rice, then demand for potatoes will suffer. The fish and chip shop example is also a good illustration of another influence — derived demand. If the demand for fish declines, so will the demand for potatoes. This will also have an effect on the demand for cooking oil, batter products, wrapping paper, frying equipment, shop premises and a whole lot of other things.

Pricing in any market is a complex juggling act requiring an understanding of all the above factors and how they affect that particular product and market. To make things worse, these demand forces are in a constant state of flux and the smaller business owner or manager will need to constantly review his pricing policy. Outside economic factors must also be considered — the days of price increases blindly following inflation have gone, but the state of the economy is a major influence and must be understood. Levels of disposable income affect some firms more than others; those in luxury goods are most susceptible to these changes, but the definition of a luxury item is constantly changing.

There is always a competitor, direct or indirect, willing to hold prices, or even to cut them, in order to steal an advantage over rivals in times of increasing prices.

A firm's overall marketing effort may also affect demand (in its own sphere of interest) and this will have an influence on pricing policy. A company putting over a high quality image, building a reputation for itself and its products, will often be able to command a premium price for its products. The same is true of well known and well liked products, although it is expensive to promote a wide enough appeal for popularity to influence price. Indeed, often smaller businesses can quickly penetrate certain profitable sections of a market dominated by large firms with huge marketing budgets by competing directly on price. Another significant factor is service – the large electrical discount houses charge minimum prices but are often out-sold by local retailers offering better service.

The smaller business owner or manager should consider his product/market strategy (see Chapter 12) and the effect that it has on his pricing policy. The position of any product in its life-cycle will have a bearing on the price of that product. If a business is going for new markets with a new product, its pricing tactics will be quite different to one aiming to penetrate an existing market further. Channels of distribution affect price; while they are needed to present products to the market, these intermediaries do need payment. The business owner or manager will have to weigh up the relative merits, in terms of price, between a 'push' campaign through direct selling and a 'pull' campaign through advertising and sales promotion.

WHAT THE MARKET WILL BEAR

There are very few businesses whose products or services stand alone, free of any competition. It is possible in very specialist technical fields, and here pricing is always the subject of intense negotiation, the only reference base being costs. In all other cases, pricing policy must contain an element of what the market will bear and in some, the market will be the only reference point used.

In certain businesses the market dictates price in a way that forces all firms operating in the sector to follow. Commodities are obvious examples, but philatelists operate within a regime which means that customers are as aware of prices as the dealers. Motor car prices – new and used – follow a fairly fixed pattern with the publication, Glass's Guide, acting as a 'bible' for car salesmen. Even these trades that follow a fairly fixed pricing system (determined by the market) still allow a degree of flexibility to the individual firm to respond to local markets by offering special deals.

Most businesses do not, however, operate within such a tidy routine – there will be many more product variations and market factors which distort pricing policy and all firms will need to refer to the market. This will mean regular market investigation and monitoring, either on an *ad hoc* basis or, better still, through an organised information system. Markets are in a continuous state of change and to enable him to meet varying price requirements, the smaller business owner or manager will need a reliable and comprehensive input of information.

Firstly, the business owner must have some idea of total demand and the pattern of that demand. Next, he or she will need to determine, accurately, how the company is performing and whether its trends match the overall picture. The competition should be studied and, taking into account product and other marketing factors, the business owner must judge how effectively his or her company is operating in the market. An understanding of customer attitudes towards the firm's prices is vital, and salesmen should be asked to monitor all customer complaints and other useful reports.

Once armed with all relevant information, the business owner or manager can construct his pricing strategy. It will be based on one of three options: meeting the competition, pricing above the competition or pricing below it. (The competition in these terms are major competitors, not every single one of them). The strategy chosen will depend on the facts collected and how they relate to the overall objectives set out in the marketing plan. The level of price compared to competitors should always be the result of strategic choice and not of mere chance.

Price may be used to reinforce an image of quality or service or it can be cut right back (together with other elements of the product 'package') as part of an effort to compete aggressively in the marketplace. Most firms tend towards a 'meeting competition' strategy, especially smaller

businesses, as this is the safest option and the owners do not
believe they are strong enough in the market to influence
price. While this is undoubtedly the safest strategy, some of
the greatest business success stories have come from small
firms rapidly expanding because they have grabbed the
pricing nettle and taken on local markets in a spectacular way.

COST-PLUS

The most popular and easiest pricing policy is simply to add a
fixed margin onto the cost price of any product. It sounds
straightforward and, for certain businesses like retailers and
wholesalers, can work very well in practice. The main problem is that a firm's costs have no relation whatsoever to what
the market will bear, i.e., how much customers are willing to
pay. There is another major problem – exactly how to
establish the costs and which base to use when you have
found them.

While reference to the market is a much better base on
which to form pricing policy, many firms use a cost-plus
system. This is probably because cost information is readily
available, whereas it is much more difficult to establish facts
about competition, markets and consumer attitudes. There is
no doubt, however, that the best pricing policy for the
smaller business is to look at costs and margins and then
consider market criteria before reaching a final pricing
decision.

On the face of it, cost information would seem easy to
collect and to quantify. Unfortunately, accounting systems
vary and problems lie in allocating certain costs to individual
products. For example, in a workshop where several items are
being produced, the division of production costs is difficult.
Also, allocating marketing costs and overheads causes problems. If the business owner or manager uses a total cost
method – allocating all costs to individual products – a distorted view of what price needs to be charged to cover these
total costs is very likely to occur.

A much better basis of cost analysis is to use marginal, or variable costing. Under this system, costs are divided into two distinct categories: fixed and variable. Fixed costs include salaries, overheads and depreciation and, as the name suggests, remain constant whatever sales are made. Variable costs are those directly related to sales and include raw materials, salesmen's commission and production costs.

Under the marginal costing system, variable costs can be directly related to sales and a figure representing the difference between sale price and the variable cost per unit can be found. This sum is then considered to represent a contribution towards fixed costs. In a business offering a range of products, the performance of each line can be accurately monitored by judging its contribution to fixed costs. When a figure for profits is added to the fixed costs and a break-even point established, the business is using the cost-plus method of pricing.

The break-even point is a vital calculation for the smaller business owner or manager wishing to use cost-plus as a method of fixing price. Breakeven is reached where total costs equal total sales revenue. If a figure for total costs is found, the price can be determined as the total sales revenue divided by unit sales. Using marginal costing, the break-even point may be found using the following equation:

$$\text{Break-even point} = \frac{\text{Total fixed costs}}{\text{Unit contribution to fixed costs}}$$

By estimating the demand for a product, having established total fixed costs, the price of the product will be the unit contribution required plus the variable cost per unit.

USE OF PRICING IN MARKETING POLICY

The break-even calculation is a useful device in that it provides an idea of the minimum price a firm may charge for its products. A further problem, however, comes from the dimension of time. Does the company wish to break even within months, after the first year, or after several years? Clearly, if a firm only has one product it will need to break even sooner rather than later. Firms with a range of products may require one line to be continued for reasons other than to provide a contribution to profits. Once the break-even point has been reached, the contribution of each additional sale becomes pure profit, unless further fixed costs are needed to maintain production. These are known as marginal profits and allowance must be made for them in terms of time and the product life-cycle.

Marginal profits are extremely important to the business owner or manager. Although he should build a profit element into the variable costs, it is only at this stage that he will receive any substantial return on investment. Once the break-even point has been reached, the business owner or manager has much more flexibility in his tactical marketing policy. He will have more funds available for direct or indirect marketing activity and he may wish to promote sales through the use of discounting.

Discounts are basically reductions in the standard price offered to certain people in order to promote sales. They are very powerful weapons and are used throughout business by companies large and small. It is important to distinguish between the *trade discount*, which is the discount offered to intermediaries on recommended retail price and merely represents intermediaries' income, and *quantity discounts*. A trade discount is not a marketing tool (although changing it may be).

Quantity discounts are offered by most businesses in an effort to persuade consumers or other businesses to maintain high levels of stock. Discounts on quantity are valuable

especially when a firm is dealing in a competitive market
with very large purchasers, or as part of a special promotional
campaign. The biggest danger lies in encouraging over-
stocking, which can distort the smooth flow of sales and, if
taken too far, can alienate customers. Some businesses offer
cash discounts or discounts for prompt payment which are
used to improve cash flow and minimise bad debts. *Seasonal
discounts* are used to improve the sale of products during
'off-peak' periods and again are often associated with a special
promotion. Summer and Winter Sales, seen each year in the
High Street, are forms of seasonal discounting.

Pricing policy is a marketing responsibility; firms that
allow accountants and production people to determine levels
of price are asking for trouble. It forms an integral part of
marketing planning and should be seen as a key element of
the business's marketing strategy. The best policy is to base
price on a sensible cost analysis and then look round at what
the market will bear. It comes right back to the basic principle of marketing which is to put the customers first, and
then to do everything possible to meet their needs.

PRICING

CHECKLIST

1 In your business, are there any market leaders that set prices and do you follow them?

2 If you are operating in a market with price leaders, have you considered using a different price strategy to 'cream off' parts of the market?

3 Are you aware of your major competitors, and what pricing policy they follow?

4 Can you list all direct, substitute and derived competitors to all your products?

5 What is the attitude of your customers to your prices?

6 Should you use pricing to project a quality image, or should you be competing aggressively on price — and are you?

7 Have you a planned pricing policy of:
   a) meeting competition;
   b) pricing above competition; or
   c) pricing below competition,
                          and do you follow it?

8 Do you use a system of variable costing to establish the profit contribution each of your products should be making?

9 Are you aware of the break-even point of each of your products?

10 Do you use pricing as an integral part of your overall marketing strategy?

11 Do you know if your business is making marginal profits, and if so, are you using them to offer discounts or to improve your marketing activities?

PART VI
Planning

XYZ PLASTICS LIMITED

ANNUAL MARKETING PLAN

1983

XYZ PLASTICS

The Marketing Plan

Smaller businesses face special difficulties when it comes to marketing; resources are scarce, management time is often over-committed, and buying in expertise from elsewhere, even if it is available, is too expensive. On the other hand, small firms do have the advantage of being closer to their customers and to the market, and can usually respond more quickly to changes than their larger counterparts.

Getting it right is the problem, and business owners and managers can only get it right by using the very best information, by planning ahead and adding enterprise – the magic ingredient. Planning is not just for next week! A successful business will not only have a marketing plan for the current year, but a pretty good idea of where it is going in three or even five years.

Setting objectives comes first. Does the company want to grow? If so, by how much? Should it increase its product range or consolidate on the most successful lines? Is there any potential for exporting, or should the home market be tied up first? Push/pull? Skim or penetrate? Quality or price competitiveness? Horizontal or vertical diversification, or retraction? Objectives take into account the possible, likely changes in technology, market tastes and sizes, the aspirations of the owners and the limitations of the workforce. Wandering through commercial life with no objectives will get you nowhere – fast!

Marketing planning should knit together the different elements of the marketing mix into a cohesive programme of development, meeting the objectives set. A standard format should be adopted. This will eliminate the risk of overlooking any aspect of the operation, no matter how small. The marketing plan should bring the various activities together, ensuring their compatability and avoiding duplication. Many companies have launched themselves into a grand promotional campaign only to find that they have not planned for the sales and distribution resources required to meet a great surge in demand.

The plan itself should start by outlining the present position, how the company fits into the market, and relevant parts of recent history. Drawing from the overall objectives set by the owner, the plan should go on to specify the marketing goals, targets and forecasts. Next comes the hard stuff – the plan of action. This should be divided into the various functions and sub-divided into the component parts of these functions, ensuring that every conceivable activity is represented. Budgets and resource requirements should be drawn together and placed at the end of the report making sure that one person is not doing one hundred and one jobs at the same time and that the total budget is somewhat less than the National Debt. Conclusions must be drawn, forming the basis of the marketing strategy to be applied over the period. Once reached, conclusions should be listed in the logical order and should always be attached at the beginning of the plan.

It goes without saying that the plan must be written down and should take the form of a well-presented report. The writing down in itself will be a major contribution to effective marketing planning, but once complete, the plan must not be filed away, never again to see the light of day. It should become the grubbiest of all documents, seen permanently on the desk of the Managing Director (and Marketing Director, if the firm has one). Permanent use is the only way to obtain full benefit from all the effort put into producing the plan, and it will require regular revision as outside influences play their parts.

Planning should ensure the most effective use of limited resources; with a valid marketing plan a business is much more likely to survive the intense competition of modern day business, and to obtain the finance necessary for its operation. The time, cost and effort expended in effective planning are more than repaid by the long term benefits of increasing performance and efficiency

SETTING OBJECTIVES

For examples of non-specific and non-quantifiable objectives, look at the articles and memorandum of any limited company. Reference is made to the reason for the company being set up — known as the objects of the company — which are masterpieces of meaningless objectives written in such a way as not to present any barriers to companies who wish to develop their activities. There is nothing wrong with the way these phrases are worded — they are designed to do a job and they do it well.

But if these are the only terms of reference within which a company operates, then it is not going to get very far. Objectives set by a business must be designed to provide a proper framework for the owner or manager to base his company's development on and, as such, must be realistic, specific and quantifiable.

There is some confusion as to the place marketing objectives have in relation to other corporate objectives. The answer is simple — they are one and the same thing. A marketing-oriented business will set its objectives on its customers' needs and the general aspirations of the owner or board of directors will take second place. Objectives will include, for example, plans for profits and other financial considerations, diversification, land and company acquisition, as well as specific short and longer-term marketing activities. But they are all rooted in the market and the business will try to meet them using effective marketing techniques.

Objectives, once set, are not immutable. Some are only for the short term: 'To gain a 5% increase in sales through a local door-to-door leaflet drop'; but 'To gain market leadership in stainless steel meat carving dishes within three years' is an example of a longer-term objective. Like the rest of the marketing plan, however, objectives should be regularly reviewed and, when circumstances change, then they should be amended. Many longer-term objectives appear on the annual marketing plan in revised form year after year.

As objectives are set with reference to the marketplace and the company's position within it, the business owner or manager will have to collect a certain amount of information *before* he starts. If the company has an information system (as outlined in Chapter 3), all the following information should be readily available.

● Market size and trends, and a good idea of anything likely to affect the market or products during the next few years
● Competitors, who they are and how they are performing in terms of market share, corporate development and marketing activities
● A full picture of how the company has performed over the past few years and how it has achieved success or experienced failure. This is especially important if the company has taken over, or merged with, another business during the previous year. An accurate report on the company's current resources is also vital – if technical expertise is very specialist, for example, and is already fully stretched, it is going to take time to find new people with the necessary skills and to train them; rapid expansion will not be possible.

● Reports from all key managers, including forecasts and budgets, outlining the problems they are experiencing are important for firms with more than a few staff. These will be needed for constructing the plan, but the owner or manager should have them before objectives are set.

● Information on customers should be available as a matter of course. Attitudes to products, pricing, marketing methods and back-up service must be monitored on a permanent basis, but it is well worth a special effort just before the objectives are set.

Throughout this book we have discussed the importance of planning, time and time again. The essence of planning is to have clear objectives and then to work out the best way of achieving them. Apart from overall company objectives, more specific ones must be set for pricing policy, product/market strategy, future sales, promotional campaigns, channels of distribution, corporate image and many other things. An understanding of what can be achieved through *effective marketing* is a prerequisite, but taking a marketing approach to running your business starts with effective planning.

PREPARING THE ANNUAL MARKETING PLAN

Within the framework of the company's overall objectives, the marketing plan sets out, in a logical way, how the business will develop. It has been said that a plan is basically three things:

1 Where the company is — present position
2 Where it is going — objectives
3 How it is going to get there — plan of action.

Quite simply, that is all the marketing plan is.

In the modern world of business it is no longer good enough for the owner of a business to carry the marketing plan around in his head. A marketing plan must be a document, and it must be a well-prepared and well-presented document. It has to be read, understood and used, and it will stand a much better chance of success if it is respected by all who come in contact with it. On a more practical note; it will normally be the second most important document as far as the bank and other financiers are concerned, and the new business will find life much easier if it has a well-researched and thought-out plan presented in a professional way. The illustration at the front of this chapter gives an idea of how a marketing plan should look. Logo, corporate colours and style must be followed; attention to detail separates the men from the boys.

Conclusions – the strategy

Conclusions should always appear at the beginning of a plan – straight after the title page and list of contents. Certain readers will only want to see the broad strategy (all will use this section to provide an initial opinion) and will not want to wade through the document searching for the relevant parts. Listed logically, and following the main sections of the plan, conclusions should be drawn and the associated strategy outlined. For example: 'The market for our plastic mouldings is very price sensitive. Last year we reached break-even on our main product of kitchen unit handles. This year we shall reduce our prices by 10% and absorb the forthcoming raw-material increases. This will allow us to considerably under-cut our closest competitor who has just invested in a new factory site.'

Drawing these conclusions together should provide the reader with a full picture of the firm's marketing strategy and contradictions must be spotted and ironed out. This section should not be cluttered with too many arguments, facts and figures, but should go straight to the point. Readers requiring more information on any particular matters will be able to go elsewhere in the plan.

Objectives, forecasts and targets

A full statement of the company's objectives should appear next. These will be drawn from overall objectives and more specific ones will come from the text of the plan. The specific marketing objectives will include a detailed analysis of sales and other forecasts, and an outline of the most important statistical data concerning markets, sales, profits and distribution.

Plan of action

This section of the marketing plan goes into the detail of every individual aspect of the company's marketing activities. It should include all relevant facts and figures – past, present and future – and put forward a logical argument for the proposed tactical and strategic plans for the coming year. The best way to approach writing this section is to imagine that the bank manager (or other interested non-employee) is to read the plan without the opportunity to ask any supplementary questions. If, after reading the plan, the bank manager was asked to advance finance, would he have enough information to make a decision? If the answer is no, the plan is not comprehensive enough.

The plan of action is the main body of the plan and, as such, should cover each of the functions of marketing. The simplest method of ensuring that nothing is left out is to follow the broad divisions of marketing (as outlined in this book) and then to sub-divide them as appropriate for your particular business. There will be four main divisions:

- Marketing research
- Sales and distribution
- Advertising and sales promotion
- Product policy

Under product policy, for example, sub-titles such as pricing policy, new product development and product/market strategy will appear.

Once the pattern has been set, each annual plan should follow a similar format. Not only does it help eliminate the risk of missing something, but it allows easy cross-reference with previous years. It is worth emphasising the value of covering each topic fully. The human memory is not exactly infallible, and even the best ones forget with alarming speed. By having all relevant information and the reasoning behind decision-making recorded in one place, the whole process of control and analysis becomes easier.

Budgets and resources

It is important to pull all the financial information together in one section of the marketing plan. It will eliminate embarassing duplication of resource allocation and puts the entire operation within a financial framework. There is always a conflict between what business would like to spend on marketing and what is actually possible. In large companies this often results in a war of attrition between marketing departments and the financial director. In the smaller business this control is not always there. The business owner or manager who discusses his marketing plan with his accountant before launching his company into a new marketing strategy, is a very wise one.

The most useful financial tool for the marketing-based businessman is undoubtedly the budgeted cash flow analysis — one should always be included in the marketing plan. This analysis brings together all sales forecasts and predicted expenditure budgets into a month-by-month projected profit and loss account, based on cash flow. The structure for this account is outlined in Chapter 3; each aspect of marketing income and expenditure is extracted and a budgeted figure entered for the month in which the bill will have to be paid, or income received. Totals are made for the month in question, and a cumulative sum gives the year-to-date figure.

Using this framework, the business owner or manager can

foresee periods of stress, and times when he may have extra resources available for special campaigns. Providing the product range is not too large, or the business too complex, marginal costing (Chapter 13) can be applied to the budgeted cash flow and a very accurate picture can be made of how the business needs to perform.

Longer-term plans

It is rarely possible for smaller businesses, especially new ones, to make specific plans for several years ahead. Although the owner or manager must have a general idea of where his business is going, the three or five-year plan common in larger companies is just not possible. Small firms are very dynamic, they are open to all sorts of outside influences, and are susceptible to dramatic change from chance happenings.

However, the annual marketing plan should contain a reference to the longer-term future of the business. This will normally be restricted to general objectives and a few comments on possible trends. This section not only gives readers a fuller picture of the business in action, but gives managers a reference point for the future.

Using the plan

The format outlined above is only a suggested way to construct the annual marketing plan. There are many variations, but they will all include the basic elements in one form or another. The important thing is actually to produce a plan (going through the work required provides an immeasurably valuable exercise in clear thinking) and then to use it. While it is true that a marketing plan is of value in approaching the bank manager, that is not its main purpose. It is an indispensible tool for *effective marketing* management and for the control of those activities involved.

During a trip in space a craft may be piloted by an

astronaut or by a computer; but behind the scenes there are many men and machines controlling the whole operation. In 'Mission Control' they are fully aware of the objectives and have an intricate plan of how they should be achieved. Control's job is to report the moment there is any deviation from the planned schedule. Space shots show control at its most sophisticated, but the same principles apply just as much to running a smaller business as they do to flying in space. The marketing plan is the instrument by which the business owner or manager can apply effective control.

The moment a business goes off course it is the job of executive management to bring it back as soon as possible. Using a plan can quickly indicate that a business is deviating from its objective course — but only if it is followed as a source of constant reference — this is merely good business practice. Business starts and finishes with its customers, establishing their needs and meeting them through planned, controlled, professional and *effective marketing.*

Index